# Breaking The Chains of Fear for Self-Healing

By

Osaze Bey

# About The Book Cover

The cover image of this book was created by Osaze Bey and designed by Princellia Hampton. The seven swirling colors represent the energy fields within every human being. These fields mirror the sun's energy but in a glorious form of nerve groups along the spinal column which empowers the body, this energy will never die once fertilization takes place because it's universal law; every life is chosen because this power can't be overruled, the only thing that will attempt to defeat it is a lie.

Everyone who looks at the cover sees an image of themselves—the life force energy within and the seat of the Spirit of God. This energy is fueled by the crown chakra, located at the top of the head, violet and white in color, and known as the highest level of spiritual consciousness. Christ reached this level, often called the violet flame. Which is why Yeshua said he and the Father are one. This life force is the origin of all living things that reside within the human body. This is the greatest power on earth and it's within you.

The yellow, radiant suns symbolize the beginning and eternal nature of every human life. We came from glory to live, mature and become our Divine self—the purpose we are meant to fulfill. Every situation and challenge in life pushes us toward that spiritual self, the eternal glory within us—the brightest light that cannot be hidden. You are looking at the inner image of self.

Peace and blessings to you. May love, truth, peace, freedom, and justice be multiplied within you—the Divine principles that guide human existence. The colors point towards spiritual consciousness, stirring wisdom, energy and maturity.

Just as we must feed our bodies with energy-rich foods, we must also feed the soul righteousness. We do this by balancing the positive and negative influences we allow into our minds, reconditioning our thoughts, and taking actions that lead to better outcomes for ourselves and others.

# Preface

*Breaking The Chains of Fear for Self-Healing* is a book of seventeen chapters, including the cover explanation, Preface, and gratitude pages. These chapters hold the true history of my life—the moments that created psychological fear from childhood into adult life. I had to learn responsibility. Through it all, I had to stand on courage.

My fear began with dyslexia and the belief that I would die young from a hereditary disease passed down from my mother through her father. It affects the cerebellum, slowly degenerating the nerves until they become uncontrollable starting from the legs to the mouth followed by death. None of my siblings lived past their forties. I don't believe I'd be alive today if I weren't my uncle's son. Four of the children born to the man I thought was my father died from that same disease. His DNA couldn't protect them from what was hidden in my mother.

I survived because I'm part of a chosen generation—one allowed to see heavenly beings and things too glorious to fully describe. I once saw a crystal city, bright as sunlight, rising upward with a gentle roar that vibrated through my entire body. I trembled—not with fear, but with awe. I couldn't move... and I didn't want to.

As a child, I thought I would die because of my memory problems. Three of my brothers and a sister were born with the disease. My sister passed at birth, and one brother died at forty-three from heart complications. My dad had a daughter by another woman, she lived in Alabama, I don't recall what city, her name was Denise Womble. We found out about her when she passed away from liver complications in her late twenties. Although we never met her, Mitchell and I drove to her funeral and met her mother. We were so distant I don't recall her name.

I didn't like myself. I rejected myself. I didn't want to be me. I don't know how I survived the battle taking place inside a mind nobody else could see. I hid within myself with no way out except through myself. I had to learn to love me.

That mindset created deep low self-esteem and constant negative thoughts, fueled by rejection. My stories show how I survived by living through the blueprints of others without understanding or accepting my own personality. I had to learn self-love by embracing the principles already within me. Fear gripped me early—violence in the neighborhood, darkness everywhere, and being raised by my mother and grandmother.

The bullying from my older brothers terrified me, especially in the environment we lived in. I experienced convulsions and high fevers. I'd wake up screaming, trembling from dreams I thought were demons coming for me. Combined with my memory struggles—spelling that never stuck, numbers running together, losing focus or getting sleepy whenever I studied—it was exhausting. Even preparing ministry messages took longer because I had to fight off sleep. Sometimes it took twenty minutes just to get through a paragraph. I fought constant frustration.

Yet when I read the Bible, something in me connected. I sensed it was more than what the systematic church presented. Certain scriptures made sense to me instantly.

They spoke to me, sometimes slowing me down, sometimes pulling me inward, but always opening my understanding. As a child, I didn't know how to ask for help; shame kept me silent. I didn't realize I was normal. I was born with the mind I have, and it's impossible to be beyond what God created you to be from conception. That makes us all unique, yet equal through Yeshua's will.

Some people are geniuses, some have photographic memory, some are more basic. Everything comes down to capacity, but we are all the same within. Throughout this book, I remembered who I am. I had to remember that people loved me, even though I spent a lifetime feeling hated. I endured jealousy and envy from people I didn't know while looking down on myself. But I remained unbroken because the love within me was stronger. I rejected that love at first, thinking it made me weak, but it saved me once I became conscious of my true self.

As an adult, I was blessed with people like Brennan Guy and the late Bro. Ka El Bey. Being surrounded by the right people helped break the chains that bound me—along with my faith in Christ. By ninth grade, I sensed a purpose from God, a feeling deep within my mind. I just couldn't fully accept it because it made me feel vulnerable. I couldn't retain anger, I hated that feeling.

The presence of Emmanuel (God with us) Spirit guided me throughout my life and taught me to love myself regardless of how others felt toward me. I didn't understand self-value until I lived through the events in these chapters. Those moments prepared me to heal from within. Now I help heal to empower the souls of all living things. Every chapter in this book is written to help someone cross the bridge of life more easily than I did. I didn't become free from myself until adult life. Love was always hidden within me, waiting for the moment I was finally ready to accept who I am.

Don't be afraid to fail. I hope this book helps you feel better about yourself.

These stories aren't written to expose others—they're written to heal. Healing requires a story, a path, a progression. This world must be healed one person at a time if we're going to survive. This book is part of that survival, helping people heal from their own self-destruction. I realized I was destroying myself, yet something within me kept pushing me to live—to live well enough to heal myself first, I knew I needed healing.

Throughout the book, I included examples from my life-coaching program, *Da Inner-Healing Gym*, and its self-healing method, The Shadow Program. I inserted them at the end of certain chapters to show how they would've helped me then, just as they help me now, psychologically.

The idea for The Shadow Program came from understanding how the mind works. Wherever you are, because of rays of light upon the body, it casts a shadow you can't get rid of. You ignore it because you're used to it. The mind is the same—designed to store life events as memories that never disappear. But the emotional weight attached to those memories can be removed through the program within you.

After receiving the first edited version of this book the editor completed 117 original pages without my knowledge which coincided with the 17 chapters I completed without planning, I stopped when I became empty of writing for at least eight months. Adding 1+7=8. The numbers code to this book are 1,7, and 8. I researched the following significance of those numbers Biblically as well: Number 1 is a cornerstone. It's the genesis, the starting point. Beginning, unity, and wholeness. religionwriters.com. Number 7: Is a representation of completing a task and also perfection. auntyflo.com. It's also associated with luck and spirituality Number 8: New beginnings, resurrection, and new creation. The number 8 symbolizes harmony, peace, and balance. It is often associated with balance, power, and success, symbolizing the harmony between material wealth and spiritual growth. guarding-angel-reading.com and azdictionary.com. The stories written in this book and my Shadow Program are a mirror image of this number definition which was discovered after I completed writing. The Shadow Program consists of four steps, the first condition is you must care, step one- courage, step two- pure love, step three truth, and step four value.

Thank you for reading this book. May your spirit be blessed by it. May it help you begin your journey toward self-healing. And if you're already healed, use your healing to help someone else. This book is meant to build lives, not break them. And if it breaks anything, let it be only so those lives can be restored to its fullness.

# Gratitude Page

This page is dedicated to the people who helped bring value to my life—knowingly and unknowingly. Thank you. My leaders and teachers were:

**1. The late John Penny**

John taught me the power of faith—speaking it, living it, and loving Emmanuel's (God's) people through Yeshua (Jesus Christ.) *"Now faith is the substance of things hoped for, the evidence of things not seen"* (Hebrews 11:1 KJV) was one of his favorite verses. I would've given up had I not seen the goodness of the Lord through John and his wife, Melissa.

**2. Pastor Glen Anderson**

Pastor Anderson opened his heart and his ministry at Forest Drive Baptist Church to help heal me and my family as we transitioned out of a demonic situation. He always kept an open door for me, privately meeting with Minister Leland Davis, whose prophetic wisdom kept me from fighting a man in his home fifteen years later as I applied his words.

**3. The late Sis. Victoria Hampton**

Owner of Seven Rays Book Store in Columbia, S.C., and teacher of the Mighty I AM Discourse. She introduced me to Saint Germain, the I AM activity, and the Violet Flame, the Christ energy of the crown chakra. She welcomed me into her store during my search for spiritual growth and accepted me as I was. It felt like we had known each other before we ever met. We agreed that everyone is the same inwardly, though religion, politics, and family values often divide us. She cared deeply about the truth. We agreed that religion was being used as a weapon to lead people from spiritual truth.

**4. The late Minister Leland Davis**
A chosen man of God who opened his private life to me the night we first met—broken and weeping from pain at home. That trust taught me how to truly listen to people's souls. Three years later, Pastor Anderson arranged another private meeting where Minister Davis spent hours helping me understand my visions and spiritual life. He remembered how my presence once helped him release his psychological pain. I could feel him drawing strength from me as he shared, and by the end, he smiled again.

**5. Ministers Robert and March Vanlue**
They prayed for guidance before asking my family and me to join their church. Pastor Robert asked me to come in as Assistant Pastor while March led worship. We knew it was time to leave Forest Drive Baptist Church and help build something new—not for titles, but because my soul needed development. After a year, as the ministry grew,

they ordained me Prophet of Truth. Through Union Bible Fellowship, I learned to value myself. It was the right move for our family.

**6. Sensei Rod Gardner**

Teacher and owner of DOJO NISHI. Sensei Gardner taught Shuri-Ryu Karatedo and welcomed me into his home, dojo, and life. I trained for seven years, earning my first-degree black belt under Sensei Gardner, Sensei Dave Chestnut, and Dr. Jimmy A. Duensing, Shodan and Sensei Van Buren.

I remember the uneasy feeling my first night—seeing Confederate flags and knowing his heritage. I wondered what I was doing there. But Sensei Gardner honored the good in his lineage. He didn't hate anyone; he was often misunderstood for embracing his heritage. He chose to live the true acts of Yeshua (Christ.) He accepted my family and me as his own.

One evening, he stopped class and had everyone sit. He asked me to stand on a sheet of paper, then another. Each time he asked if I had "gained height." When I finally said yes, he told me: *"Never despise small achievements. One thin sheet at a time, you rise. Look back one day and see how far you've come."* I love that Confederate man for the life lessons he placed within me.

**7. Dean Graziosi and Tony Robbins**

Creators of Mastermind.com, empowering people to use their gifts to empower others. I completed a Tony Robbins life coaching course and am part of Dean's inner circle. They've changed millions of lives, including mine.

**8. Jim Kwik**

The world's number one brain coach. In 2018, an online program led me to one of his sessions on memory and learning. At the end, he said something that changed my life: *"People learn at different speeds. It doesn't mean something is wrong—you were born the way you are. Accept who you are and find what works for you."* Those words filled my heart with joy. They helped break the shame I carried about my short memory.

**9. Hamel and Isis El Bey**

They ordained me as Chief in their Seminole Indian tribe council, previously located in Charlotte, N.C. They taught us how to use Case Law also.

**10. Ordination into the Moorish American National Government Divine Ministry**

I was ordained by Grand National Chairman Sheik Elihu N. Pleasant-Bey, author of *The Exhuming of a Nation*. I was appointed National Representative for the Office of Education and Truth. Spiritual truth has followed me all my life. Just as Sensei Gardner honored his heritage, I, too, had to learn to honor the principles I was born with—even the meekness I once rejected within myself.

**11. Nikki van de Sanden**

Founder of The Journey and an excellent life coach. I joined her school and completed her High-Ticket Coaching Offers That Sell 5-Day Challenge and her one-page offer training. She's a wonderful person who overcame her own brain challenges and now helps others with passion and purpose.

**12. Dr. Hendo I. L. Henderson**

Ad hoc judge of The Universal World Court. His conference calls are spiritually empowering and reconnect people to Divine bloodlines—an identity many have forgotten. His teachings help restore that connection by being Indexed to Identify who you are and whose you are, serving one hundred and ninety eight nations. *"The earth is the Lord's, and the fulness thereof; the world, and they that dwell therein"* (Psalm 24:1).

**13. My gratitude also goes to the women and men invited into my residence during difficult moments in their lives.**

A woman whose apartment burned called me after

losing almost everything. She stayed a night or two while finding help. Though temptation existed, I refused to take advantage of her vulnerability. She needed safety, not added regrets from me.

**14. I invested in an audio book titled, The Prosperous Coach by Steve Chandler and Rich Litvin. Two of the most successful Life Coaches.** The information in that book wasn't too complicated. It gave me an advanced understanding of a life coach's life and of how important it is to value customers above everything else; because trust is the key for everyone including the administrative part of life coaching.

**15. Dr. Business, DB:** WDRB Media/ WGIV the Soul of Charlotte radio station Charlotte, NC. helped me create my radio show, Da Wolf's Pray Lo Radio. They encourage entrepreneurship.

Another woman, verbally and physically abused by her husband, called me late one freezing night after he beat her and threw her out. She and her child stayed in my spare room. She said it was the best sleep she'd had in a long time because of the peace in my home.

Two men, on separate occasions, came to me about being abused by their wives. Hearing that was a shock—I only know women being physically abused. As we talked, we explored who they were as men and why they chose partners who dominated them. It took courage for them to admit their suffering. I learned to give balanced advice and to never add to a client's pain. Trust is sacred.

To every person who has been abused, controlled by fear, or felt imprisoned in their own homes—even by respected family members or community leaders: your cries were heard by the Creator. Your tears were stored in heaven.

When you felt manipulated, confused, or unable to find rest, hope still lived within you. That hope was Emmanuel's (God's) presence. Even when you felt forgotten, Emmanuel did not leave you. His love kept you when you didn't have the strength to keep yourself.

A special thanks to the people that didn't just stand by me, they were instrumental for the success of this book: Rebecca W. Evans, Dr. Ronald Payne, Sr. (AKA Good Foot the Clown), my Brother and business partner from India, Gautam Kumar, Diamond Johnson, Editor, Princellia (Conna) Hampton, book cover design, Dr. Amy Durso, Forensic Pathologist.

# Table Of Contents

Chapter 1 — Wheeler Hill: The Origin of My Fears....**1**

Chapter 2 — The First Day of School: Blueprint of My Life....**12**

Chapter 3 — The Move From Wheeler Hill....**18**

Chapter 4 — I Found Out I Wasn't My Dad's Son....**30**

Chapter 5 — The Strike That Altered My Sight and Life....**40**

Chapter 6 — The Decision That Saved My Life for a Divine Purpose....**47**

Chapter 7 — The Salvation and Transformation of Billy....**56**

Chapter 8 — The Passing of Malree Placed Me as Head of Household at Age 16....**66**

Chapter 9 — The Transition Into Adult Life Became Spiritually Frustrating at Work....**73**

Chapter 10 — My Transition Into Christian Life

Added Many Challenges....**81**

Chapter 11 — My Compatible Marriage to Josie....**89**

Chapter 12 — I Wasn't Included in My Dad's Will....**99**

Chapter 13 — My Promotion Into Hell....**105**

Chapter 14 — The Shout That Changed Everything....**117**

Chapter 15 — The Miracle Chapter....**125**

Chapter 16 — Josie's Passing....**135**

Chapter 17 — My Reward....**175**

# Chapter 1 — Wheeler Hill: The Origin of My Fears

I am Osaze Bey—Sovereign Principal, Moor, Cherokee, and Catawba through bloodline, not paperwork. I was born in 1961 as Phillip M. Pittman Jr. to Reatha Pittman in Columbia, South Carolina, at the Columbia Hospital on Harden Street, formerly Richland Memorial Hospital. Later, it was named Palmetto Health Richland. Now, it goes by the name Prisma Health.

The stories in this book follow my life from conception to 2020, when I took a mind-improvement course by Jim Kwik, the world's number one brain coach. A year later, I joined Mastermind.com—the self-education movement that awakened the gift in me to become a life coach and help people heal. Everything written here is true. I share these events to empower the reader toward self-healing.

I survived my experiences by applying wisdom. If I failed at something in life I learned from it, I learned to apply peace when threatened or alone, courage when I didn't believe in myself, pure love for the souls of others when rejected or disrespected, and harmony when I was confused about who I am. Those energies became the foundation of my survival. They helped me accept myself and break the grip of inner fear.

This book and program exist to help others cross into self-acceptance and thrive—hopefully easier than I had to. People learn to get through each day, but the question is: are they thriving?

Growing up in one of the most violent areas of Columbia—Wheeler Hill—was challenging. My uncle, Joseph "Coca-Cola Joe" Nesbit Sr. also known as muscle Joe, employed by the Coca-Cola Bottling Company located in Columbia S.C., he and his family lived one block behind us. As dangerous as the area was, there was something unique about living there. Our house sat about two miles from Booker T. Washington High School, and Five Points—a busy bar and shopping area—was about a 15-minute walk.

One day, my grandmother told my brothers and me to meet her at the Winn-Dixie in Five Points. I had been outside playing in the dirt when the message came. My brother Billy ran home, gathered us, and we walked to help carry groceries because we didn't own an automobile. My grandmother, Magdalene (Maggie, Malree) Harris, was furious when she saw me covered in dust. She fussed at Billy for bringing me to the store looking like that. She pointed at the white children staring at me from their parents' cars. I was embarrassing her. My brother Mitchell (Floyd) yelled at me too.

I was always dirty from playing in the dirt—it was my favorite thing to do. I was like Pig-Pen from Charlie Brown. I didn't know any better, and although I felt bad for a moment, I got over it.

I fell in love with drums by beating sticks on boxes and trash-can lids. I'd listen to the Booker T. Washington marching band practicing in the distance and watch the church drummer whenever I sat on the front pew. The University of South Carolina football practice field was about four miles from home. At age seven, a friend and I snuck to the practice field. We jumped to swing on the sleds, the top of it came down upon my forehead causing a laceration.

We were terrified. I was bleeding, and we weren't supposed to be there. We had no choice but to go home and face a whipping. That same boy would become the first person I fought on the first day of school. My grandmother grabbed me, shaking me, yelling, “You're always getting into something!” as she wiped the blood from my head. The cut was deep—I needed three stitches from the Emergency Room.

I was between five and eight years old during our time in Wheeler Hill—too young to understand life but old enough to feel fear. I didn’t understand those emotions until years later, when I realized that daily circumstances—and the state of mind of the people around us—shape our lives.

Our house had a red tin roof that rattled loudly when it rained. Thunder shook the entire place. I was terrified, and my older brothers made it worse by telling me thunder was God being angry, I had to be good. Then I asked myself, why was God angry? Because of bad people? The house had two rooms, a bathroom, and a kitchen. It was attached to another house by adjoining bathrooms in an alley behind a church on a dead-end street. Two beds in each room. Sometimes nine people lived there. That alley was the origin of my fears.

There weren’t any lights in that alley. At night, it was pitch-black. Criminals used it as a getaway, and people used it as a shortcut to the bootleg house behind us. My brothers intensified my fear by telling me the dark shadows we saw at night were ghosts but they were people cutting through the yard. I was too young to understand what was actually happening.

One of our neighbors—a mentally unstable man—tried to break into our house to rape my mother when my grandmother wasn't home. My mother wasn't afraid. She told us—Joseph (Joe), the fourth born; John, the fifth; and me—to sit still because we were ready to bust the door down ourselves. She sat on the bed with a butcher knife in one hand and a baseball bat in the other, waiting calmly for him to break the door. The lock held, that strong door saved his life.

I was terrified. My two older brothers were gone with my grandmother, so it was just my younger brothers and me. I was eight years old and ready to fight for my mother. She was known for her strength—people said she beat up every boy who mistreated her in school and once threw a brick through a window at a woman she caught with my dad.

What blew my mind was what happened later. That same man showed up again—this time at our new place, Latimer Manor. He knocked on the door asking to talk to me. My brother asked what he wanted. He said he needed to tell me something before he moved. They asked if I wanted to go outside. I said yes. They watched from the window as we sat on a grassy hill. He told me he was my father, that he loved my mother, and wanted to take care of me. I knew he was lying—just a crazy man—but I was confused. Why me?

When I told Billy, he said, "He's a damn liar. Mama hated that man. She said she would kill him if he messed with her children." My family planned to beat him up and call the police so that he'd never come back.

A year later, that same man was on the news for murdering an insurance agent—our own agent too. He fled the state but was eventually arrested. Which is why he told me he was leaving, he just killed someone. WOW! While in jail, he met one of my grandmother's best friends and church members, he convinced her he'd changed. But once he got out, he showed his true nature again. His anger frightened her so much she filed a restraining order to keep him away from her.

Months later, she told me the man's name—only then did we realize we knew the same person. She told me how he stalked and beat her on a sidewalk in downtown Columbia until strangers stepped in and saved her. Hearing it hurt us both. Had I known earlier, I would've warned her. I already knew he was dangerous.

Among many things, our mother taught us how to defend ourselves the right way—while staying peaceful. She taught us how to fight, how to protect each other, and how to avoid violence unless absolutely necessary. Her inner peace came from love—deep, genuine love for life despite her illness. I inherited that love, but for years I rejected it. I thought love made me appear weak because some people treated me so harshly. Anger didn't sit right with me; it felt foreign. I couldn't hold on to it. I hated how anger changed people—how it changed me.

I often retreated into my own mind. I struggled with slow memory, spelling, and finding the right words  when I knew what I wanted to say. I feared being wrong all the time. People mistreated me for not being who they thought I should be. That blueprint followed me throughout life until I learned how to reclaim my power. I thought I needed fixing, but I didn't. I just needed understanding. (Path 1, Week 1: Courage; Path 4, Week 4: Value of my Shadow Program would apply here)

an incident with the City of Columbia Police Department shook our entire family. All of us children were in the yard when a stolen car sped into the alley. The driver jumped out while the car was still rolling. Four police cars followed with sirens blaring. My brother, Billy screamed for us to move. We barely got out of the way before the car rolled past us and the police barreled in behind it.

Officers jumped out with guns drawn. One fired at the driver, missing him—the bullet whizzed past my brother Joe's ear. My mother and grandmother yelled at the police for endangering our lives. The cops claimed the man stole the car and asked if we knew him. None of us would tell him although we knew him. After they left, the adults talked about how careless the police were with Black children's lives. They knew if we'd been white, the officers would've handled things differently. Back then, there was no real recourse. Only fear. Only survival with courage. (Path 3, Week 3: Truth & Clarity would apply here)

Another terrifying moment still stays in my mind. The corner store was three blocks away, so our parents trusted us to go alone. I didn't like going without a note because I'd forget what to buy. One day my grandmother sent me on an errand. On the way, I saw the bootlegger's son—a known unstable man—walking toward me with a knife. I crossed the street. He chased me. I ran under a nearby house, screaming. Two women on a porch watched everything but did nothing.

He crawled under the house after me. I was cornered by a brick column, screaming for help. As he got close—knife in hand—I kicked dirt and fought, and for some reason he turned and left. Nobody came out. Nobody checked. I climbed out shaking with fear. When I got home crying, my family knew the man, but nothing could be done. He wasn't always violent. But the fear stayed with me. (Path 1, Week 1: Courage of my Shadow Program.)

From ages five to eight, I got sick every winter—fevers, nightmares, convulsions, bronchitis. I'll never forget waking up shaking, sweating, screaming from nightmares: strange faces coming toward me in slow motion, laughing and trying to harm me. I also sleepwalked. These experiences affected my self-esteem and social development. I was the middle child and felt like I didn't fit anywhere.

My older brothers were bigger and got decent hand-me-downs. By the time clothes reached me, they were worn out or too big. I was skinny. My younger brother Joseph was almost my size but stronger, so I got his hand-me-downs too. One Christmas, all my brothers got good gifts, fruit, and candy. My mother unwrapped my gift in front of us—it was a pair of black ice skates from a white family we knew. They fit, but I couldn't walk in them. There was nowhere to ice skate in Columbia, S.C.

My brothers laughed, asking where I planned to use them. My mother said maybe North Carolina, where my dad was from, had a place. My grandmother agreed, she knew somehow I was a natural dancer. I was disappointed, but I convinced myself we'd make that trip. I hung the skates in the closet and dreamed all winter of using them. We never went, and I outgrew them. That pattern—getting close to something but not quite reaching it—kept repeating throughout my life.

The only place I found peace was lying on the ground, staring at the sky, wondering how the stars got there. I was told God and Jesus put them there, and that made me want to see them—and the "man in the moon." Malree always said, "Boy, you ain't no better than the man on the moon." Looking at the sky made me feel safe. Connected. Held.

I don't recall having a birthday party. Billy, the oldest, was always celebrated. Floyd Mitchell, the second, was big and fast—he got attention too. Joseph, born on Christmas Day, was strong despite having the same disease as our mother. John, the baby, was spoiled. I don't remember being celebrated.

The only birthday party I ever had was my fortieth, given by my late wife, Josie W. Pittman. I told her my story before we married, and she remembered. She said forty was the perfect time to celebrate me—not only because of my past, but because none of my brothers or my mother lived to see that age except Mitchell. (Path 2, Week 2: Pure Love for Self would apply

here)

# Chapter 2 — The First Day of School: Blueprint of My Life

The first day of school wasn't exciting for me at all. I went to Benson Elementary from first through third grade. My eldest brother, Billy Pittman, and my second oldest brother, Floyd, went inside after the bell rang. I ignored it because I was too busy sitting on the ground making sand mounds. At home, I loved playing outside in the dirt yard, so school wasn't enough to pull me away. I was a first grader who didn't understand the whole "transition inside the building" thing.

While I was building my sand mound, another first-grade boy I knew walked up and asked what I was doing. Then he stomped upon my mound. That one move made me jump up and fight. The principal came out, broke us up, dragged us to his office, and called our brothers in. When they arrived, the principal spanked us with a wooden paddle for fighting and not going to class. I felt like I was in a boxing match getting hit from both sides. I got punished for defending myself, and I couldn't wrap my mind around that at all.

On the way home, my two older brothers kept slapping me on my head, laughing: "You got into a fight on the first day of school! Did you win?" They reminded me of the whipping I was about to get at home because of the note the principal sent.

Sure enough, I got my butt whipped when I got home. My mother laughed, "Phillip P., you got into a fight? Oh my god!" My grandmother followed with, "Phillip P., you got into a mess on the first day of school! Why didn't you go inside?" I told her Billy said to stay in front of the school entrance because the older students went in first—besides, that boy had no business stepping on my sand mound. She still whipped me. I felt confused as hell. I had questions I couldn't ask because I knew asking would get me punished again. So all those thoughts stayed locked in my mind with no answers.

Later that school year, that same boy and I snuck away to the football field and decided to skip a class field trip. We hid in the bushes until the school bus drove away. The moment it left, we came out like geniuses. What were we thinking? The class went on a field trip, and my little first-grade self skipped school to hang out in the neighborhood. The principal found us, locked us in his office like we were in jail...lol. We were in trouble with everybody—students, teachers, parents, even the family pets were scared because we had gone missing. I got another whipping, a week of restrictions, and a ban on playing with that friend. Honestly, it helped, because every time we got together, he had "bright ideas" that sounded good but got us into trouble—including what we thought was sex with girls, even though we had no real clue or feeling for any of it but kissing.

I wasn't ready to pass first grade, so I was held back another year. That's when my dislike for school really settled in. I was dyslexic, though I didn't learn that until adult life. Reading, writing, and spelling were hard. Math was worse—the numbers ran together and made me panic. I couldn't focus. I didn't like myself and thought something was wrong with me. I struggled to accept myself but couldn't hang on to anger. I remember during that time as being deeply troubled yet held together by love.

We were a Christian family. My grandmother was a member of a Holiness church—The Bible Way Church of Atlas Road in Columbia, S.C. While we were there, my older brothers and the pastor's son bullied me. When they did, I fought back—even in church. The deacons and church mothers would pull us apart and sit me at the front like I was the troublemaker. The only good thing was that they sat me in front of the drummer. That made all my anger disappear. I loved drums. I learned to play church songs on boxes and got good at it—my brothers knew it too.

My mother was a member of Mount Sinai Holiness Church. Her pastor, the late Bishop Anderson, visited us often. He always kept a clean car. One day when he arrived and stepped out, I threw sand inside his car and tried to run. My mother covered her mouth laughing, but everyone else was furious. Bishop Anderson caught me, took off his belt, and whipped me. My grandmother made me clean the sand out of his car then made me go inside the house the rest of the day.

We grew up bouncing between churches. We had a spiritual foundation and a good family, but I had questions about things I saw in church—behaviors that didn't feel Christlike. Something felt wrong and right at the same time. We were taught to respect adults and not question them, so asking anything about church meant punishment. I felt mentally stuck with nowhere to go. I didn't think highly of myself, not knowing dyslexia was behind so many of my struggles.

Between ages five and seven—a major stage in child development—I was dealing with psychological stress, dyslexia, and low self-esteem. Girls didn't choose me. There weren't many my age, and the older ones talked down to me because I wasn't as neat as the other boys because they were older, I was called ugly. Their attitudes made me shy around girls. I wouldn't open up unless they were my age. I didn't like older girls; they were always mean to me. That early dislike became distrust of women later in life. It was a defense mechanism. I couldn't hold conversations because I didn't know what to say. I felt ashamed of myself and didn't know how to explain what I was feeling.

The only thing I really liked about myself was my laughter. I was like my mother—we loved to laugh. I looked strange to myself when I played in the mirror, twisting my body, making faces, and creating crazy sounds. I loved watching comedy shows like *Gomer Pyle* with Jim Nabors and *The Andy Griffith Show*. I watched *Groovie Goolies*, a monster rock-band cartoon from the '70s, and *Looney Tunes*—especially Foghorn Leghorn. I was fascinated by the character voices and tried to copy them. Those shows shaped my sense of humor later in life.

My uncle Bud—Fletcher Harris—lived with us until he graduated from Booker T. Washington High School. He was drafted into the U.S. Army to fight the war in Vietnam after graduation. I used to make the family laugh by mocking him in the mirror, pretending he was messing up in front of the sergeant like Gomer Pyle. We were happy when he came home on leave. He ended up not going back, and we found out when the Military Police showed up at our door asking for him. When my grandmother opened the door, I yelled, "Look, it's Sergeant Carter looking for Uncle Bud!" Everybody laughed, and Billy slapped me on the head saying, "It's the Army, not the Marines, dummy," I said, "o yeah."

Uncle Bud was the fun one in the family. He made a pipe horn he played in nightclubs and with bands. He was so good they asked him to perform with the James Brown band at the Township Auditorium in Columbia, S.C. My love for music comes from him.

Then things changed. I overheard we were moving somewhere that didn't allow pets, so we had to give away our dogs—a German Shepherd and a black Chihuahua. That was a sad day. A new kind of fear settled in my mind because everything was changing.

# Chapter 3 — The Move from Wheeler Hill

One day my brothers and I were outside playing when I noticed something was wrong in the house. My mother, father, and grandmother were arguing. I was the only one who seemed to notice, so I stopped playing and sat on the porch near the room where they were. My dad told my mother he was leaving. She was devastated because her disease was getting worse. I sat there confused and scared.

A few minutes later, a cab pulled into the yard. My dad stormed out, loaded his travel bags, and looked at me angrily without saying a word. Then he got in the cab and left. I kept telling myself he'd be back, even though I had watched him pack those bags. As the cab drove away, I turned and saw my mother through the screen door, lying across the bed crying while my grandmother held her. Through my mind I can still see her laying on her stomach across the bed crying.

My parents fought a lot. Dad was a ladies' man and did very little to support us. My mother didn't play about that. Before he left, he spent most of his time hanging around local nightclubs. Once she found out where he was, she chased him out of the club with a baseball bat. She loved him, but eventually realized he wasn't worth the pain—especially as her health continued to fail. She was torn psychologically however, she had us, we all loved her.

I don't remember much about my father being around, even though he lived with us for a while. As I got older, I didn't forget that day. My mother was heartbroken, her body weakening, and him leaving only pushed her deeper into a low mental state. Even so, she remained a strong woman with extraordinary courage.

Years later, at a family reunion in Murrells Inlet, South Carolina, I met a relative who grew up with my mother. She told me stories from when they were children. She said that when Reatha was young and healthy, she was a fine, beautiful, brown-skinned woman—strong, sharp, and the type who didn't let anyone take advantage of her. She fought back and beat any boy who tried her. She was determined, peaceful, kind, loving, full of laughter, and deeply connected to God spiritually.

I was too young to understand everything about her, but I felt her kindness and peace. I remember that clearly. I connected to her energy even when I couldn't make sense of it.

Whenever I got myself into trouble as a boy, she usually laughed. I don't remember her whipping me much—my grandmother and Uncle Bud took care of that. She knew I had issues, along with just being a regular boy who did forgetful, silly things. One moment I was blowing air through a box fan playing with metal blades while it was on. The front had a cover but the back didn't. I put my left hand on the front and my right hand behind it, and my right hand got too close to the spinning blade. It gashed the area under my second finger and blood went everywhere. At the emergency room, the doctor gave me three stitches and joked about whether I'd learned my lesson. It felt like the only time I got attention was when I was sick or injured, I saw the hospital often.

As we were preparing to move our mother's health worsened. She was employed by Master's Cleaners located in Five Points, Columbia S.C. The manager of the cleaners came to our resident to inform Malree that Reatha was too sick to continue working there but refused to leave and that she didn't want to call the police to remove Reatha. She informed Malree that mom shakes won't allow her to perform duties.

Malree thanked the manager for coming to our neighborhood before calling the police because she tried to convince Reatha not to go to work any more. But Reatha would become vocal and physically aggressive with anger not realizing she was sicker. Malree and Billy went with the manager to bring mom home which she didn't like at all. She blamed Malree for causing her to lose her job. They fought once they reached our residence. Reatha's mental status began to change, she seemed more aggressive fighting Malree every day. Malree was the only person mom was mean towards, otherwise she was peaceful about everything, her demeanor was becoming the opposite of who she was. I overheard Malree telling Billy and Mithchell she had to put mom in a nursing home that she can be taken care of because they were fighting every day. Mom believed Malree wasn't her true mother, she became vocal about that so strongly we would have believed her if we didn't live with her every day knowing she was being taken care of and protected by us, we would fight for her because she was sick.

I was eight when we moved away from Wheeler Hill. I was going into the third grade, and we were told we'd be integrating with Caucasian children for the first time. I had mixed feelings; I'd heard White people hated Black people, even though my grandmother worked as a maid for three wealthy white families—the Brutons, Bollins, and Hensels. Through them she got connected to DSS for help raising five boys and a sick daughter.

We moved to the projects, Latimer Manor, and lived in building three near the entrance. Moving was stressful; nobody knew us yet. That changed fast. Every day my mother tried to run away because she didn't want to move, and her condition was getting worse. Her balance was off, her whole body became shaky. If you didn't know her, you'd think she was drunk, but the neighborhood quickly learned who she was because she'd stop and talk with a few women along the way.

Sometimes she wandered all the way to the back of Latimer Manor about a mile away, where trouble always seemed to be happening. When we realized she was missing, I was always afraid. My two older brothers had to go look for her. When they found her, the women in the neighborhood learned she was sick. Billy and Floyd were big enough to guide her home even when she fought them—verbally and physically. Because of all that, people got to know our family quickly, Billy became popular.

The disease kept progressing. Once school started, our grandmother couldn't care for her alone, so someone from DSS came twice a week to help until mother had to be placed in a nursing home. We visited her every Sunday, uncle Joe owned a car, he would drive us. They made sure I was dressed nice and clean. I'd gotten older and wasn't rolling in dirt every day.

We kept her at home as long as we could, but eventually she became bedridden and the stress was too much. Even confined to her bed, she stayed peaceful and happy. We spent time with her daily, helping to bathe and feed her. The only person she struggled with was her mother. She didn't believe my grandmother was really her mom. When my grandmother tried to help, mom would scratch and hit her, yelling, "You not my momma." We couldn't prove any abuse was happening, but it was obvious it had become too much for my grandmother to manage alone.

Whenever I walked into my mother's room, she would laugh with me. I'd usually say or do something silly. One moment I'll never forget was when my brother Mitchell caught me standing in front of mom with my pants down. I had just discovered two hairs growing in my private area and thought I was ready to have sex, so I excitedly went to show her. Right as I pulled my pants down to ask what to do next, Mitchell walked in. He yelled at me, beat me up, and dragged me out of the room. Mom just laughed; she understood, but she didn't bother explaining anything to him. I was around nine years old.

As I grew older, I realized how important third grade was for my development. I was there physically however, my mind wasn't. I was too ashamed of my memory issues which made reading slower, and I couldn't finish classwork on time. When I couldn't focus, I bothered the person next to me—especially if they were white. I faked being sick to get out of work because I didn't do homework, and that left me lost the next day in class. My brothers had their own assignments, and my grandmother only had a third-grade education, so she couldn't help. She tried to keep us on track, but I always found something else to draw my attention.

I attended Satchel Ford Elementary, our first year integrating. A friend and I often got into trouble during recess with older white boys who harassed us. We'd retaliate, and *we* were the ones reported and labeled as the bad boys. It made me bitter, even though we caused our share of problems as well. I don't know how I passed third grade, but somehow I did. Music class was the bright spot—I came in second during a percussion memory test, and the whole class cheered. I recall being shocked they were happy for me. Something in me came alive with music that made people happy.

I wasn't a bad kid; I just didn't know how to express myself or believe in myself. My teacher eventually sent a note home asking my grandmother to take me to a child psychiatrist because I ended up in the principal's office so often. They thought I had mental issues because I was quiet otherwise. The evaluation proved otherwise. The psychiatrist wrote simple words—*house, dog, bike, colors*—flipped the paper, and asked me what I saw. The questions were so easy I felt embarrassed and took longer to answer. My grandmother wondered why it took me so long, but I was scared to question anything with her there because she would embarrass me. At the end, the psychiatrist said nothing was wrong with me.

My grandmother, being the loud storyteller she was, told everybody about the appointment—mainly how long it took me to answer, not that the doctor said I was normal. That bothered me. I already felt unsure about myself, and I had no idea how to fix anything. The only thing I trusted was a sense of peace I felt inside, even though I thought it made me weird. People labeled me slow, I started rejecting myself because of it. I forgot I was normal.

Anger scared me because it always came with consequences, so I chose peace, even though some people took advantage of that. Within, I knew I had to change, but I didn't know how. The one thing that stayed strong was my mother's love. I loved her dearly. She was amazing, even as her body declined.

We moved from one violent neighborhood to another. My two older brothers became well known because they were big and hung out in the back of the Manor, where fights, murders, and drug deals were common. There were good people too. One of the good families was the Dowlings. Floyd Dowling—who we called Buck—became my close friend from fourth grade through high school.

Buck and I bonded immediately. Neither of us liked doing homework. One week he told our fifth grade teacher he'd lost his book. When I visited his apartment I saw the book hidden behind the couch where they kept a gun. I called him out on it and we laughed. The next day I told the teacher he'd "found" it.

Buck showed up at my house one day, and I followed him around the corner to his place. I wasn't supposed to go there, and I knew I'd get in trouble if my older brothers found out. Everyone in the neighborhood knew my brothers, especially Billy. When Buck's family saw me, they said, "Hey little boy, you look like Billy Pittman." My stomach dropped—I knew Billy would hear about it and chase me home.

Floyd and I played in his living room that day. He showed me his dad's gun—a .38 pistol—and the BB rifle we later used to shoot in the woods behind the old Beltline Drive-In Theater. We used to sneak into the theater on weekends. Buck was outgoing and bold; I wanted to be that way too, but I was quiet and introverted. It felt safer. People misjudged me, and I didn't think much of myself back then.

My brothers boxed and wrestled and later played football and basketball for St. Andrews Middle School and Columbia High School. They were talented. My gifts hadn't shown up yet which made them think I was too weak. I wasn't allowed to go to the back of the Manor, and if my brothers caught me there, they'd run me home and whip my butt. They thought I was vulnerable to the older boys who bullied younger children.

I didn't get into fights except when dealing with bullies. I was quiet and peaceful, and people respected my family. Folks called me "Little Billy" because I looked like my oldest brother, and I wanted to be like him so badly I even tried walking like him. I wanted out of my own skin.

In fourth grade, I stayed out of the principal's office more, but I still didn't see the value in homework. Studying for spelling tests was hard because I couldn't remember the words. That gap from third grade followed me.

By fifth grade, my body was changing—I was taller but skinny with no muscle. That's when we discovered I had athletic ability. I had speed and loved baseball. My brothers signed me up for Pop Warner football. I played offensive and defensive tackle because of my height and dominated on the defensive line. All I knew to do was hit the player in front of me as hard as I could. I was five feet six weighing one hundred 110 pounds.

Even then, I hated how I looked. My grandmother and brothers noticed how tall I was getting, especially as my feet grew. I felt embarrassed and unattractive. I wished every day that I would stop growing. Football helped, though. My sickness and nightmares faded, even though I still sleepwalked at times. I still struggled with my memory, but I didn't understand that it wasn't a flaw—it was just part of my life but I didn't know that as a child.

I started taking responsibility for my homework, but I'd often forget to study for tests. I felt ashamed when the papers came back covered in red F's and "You did not study." I spent too much time hanging out with Floyd. Most of my homework was incomplete, and my brothers scolded me for it. My grandmother was older, but I was still young enough to get whippings with belts, switches, or anything she could reach—even in public.

But with all that, we were normal boys who stayed out of legal trouble, even without a father around. Our grandmother was enough.

# Chapter 4 — I Found Out I Wasn't My Dad's Son

By the time I reached fifth grade, our family was well known in the community. My mother was bedridden by then. One day during a visit with her, I asked why my birth certificate read *Phillip Morris Pittman Jr.*—why I was a Jr. I only noticed it because I needed the certificate to play football. She was proud of me for that.

She told me she named me after my dad's brother because she loved him. Then she showed me his picture she kept in her Bible: he was a young preacher in a black suit with a white minister's collar. She said I was skinny like him. Hearing that gave me a peaceful feeling within my soul. I didn't think deeper at the time. It just felt good knowing my dad's brother was a minister and his picture was in mom's Bible. I wondered if I were going to be a minister was my only thoughts as a child.

What I didn't understand was that she wasn't talking about an uncle—she was talking about my real father. I was too young to catch it. All I knew was I finally had something good to think about myself: I looked like him.

That was the only conversation we ever had about it. I was too young, and she was slipping away. I didn't learn the truth until adult life, after I was forced to retire early to care for my sick wife.

During this stage of my life, Mom's health kept getting worse. She trembled constantly. Before that, she could walk and interact normally, but her mouth began to quiver, and it scared us. It was the first time we saw that change. I even wondered if I might die from it too, because I always felt so different. She was the only person who understood me. I was attached to my oldest brother, Billy, too. My thoughts were shifting, my body changing, and I wasn't sick as often.

Billy was my idol. He was a junior at the old Columbia High School downtown Columbia, S.C.. He graduated in 1976. Everybody liked him—smart, athletic, cool. He was four years older than me and the best big brother you could ask for. He played two years of varsity football at five foot ten inches tall weighing two hundred ten pounds. I was playing Pop Warner, and Mitchell—who we called Floyd—was on Columbia High's B team. Floyd and I played basketball together at St. Andrews Junior High. He was the starting center, and I came off the bench when we were ahead. Basketball wasn't my favorite sport; my hands were too small, and I jammed my thumbs catching the ball. Every practice session became painful.

Billy graduated two years while Floyd was a sophomore on varsity. Floyd and I weren't close. We were okay, but not the kind of "close" brothers ought to be. Our personalities clashed. I don't remember him coming to my games. He rarely encouraged me. He always found the negative in everything. Still, he was smart. Wofford College and South Carolina State both offered him full scholarships. But at home, he was as mean as he was tough on the football field.

We were all older by then and respectful to our parents—except Mitchell (Floyd). He was mean to our grandmother because he felt she treated our mother poorly who didn't know much, especially about private matters. The best thing about her was her cooking. Her mother taught her by letting her create her own recipes. She tried to teach me, but I thought cooking was "a girl thing." She could've cooked for a living. She raised us the best she knew how, and most people loved her. In the neighborhood she was Ms. Maggie. At church she was Sister Harris. She sang with the Mothers of Bible Way Church, Atlas Road and took us to Tuesday night service. Mitchell and I always got into fights there. I hated sitting next to him.

He'd irritate our two younger brothers by blowing his nasty breath in their faces. He was tall and bigger than all of us, and that hot breath went straight up your nose. It angered anybody. At home and in public, Billy and Mitchell bullied me and my younger brothers that way. The little ones cried in church because they had to sit beside Mitchell. He was nasty in many ways—big, intimidating, and quick to hurt you if you challenged him. He got away with a lot because of his size. Billy was mostly cool with just occasional moments of disrespect, but Mitchell was ruthless every day, though smart.

One Sunday in church, he blew his breath in my face and I elbowed him. He elbowed me back in the chest—hard. I hit him again. He hit me harder. I cried because I was tired and he hurt me. I hit him back which led to a fight in church.

What made it worse was that *I* always got blamed. The ushers or deacons broke us up and moved me without asking what happened. We told Malree what Billy and Mitchell did, but she couldn't do much besides fuss. If she tried to whip them, they'd take whatever she used out of her hand and tell her it wasn't happening anymore. So I learned to fight back even though I knew I'd lose. I never bullied my younger brothers. We had normal boy moments—but

Mitchell was relentless. His demeanor changed like he didn't care what he did to people or animals he didn't like. By sixth grade he was six feet tall and two hundred pounds. By senior year, six-three and two-fifty, my senior year I was five feet nine inches one- eighty pounds.

One day, Malree wasn't home, and Mom couldn't discipline us anymore. Mitchell did something that pushed me past my limit. I ran to the kitchen, grabbed a big knife, and charged at him. When he saw me coming, he ran up the stairs. As he turned the corner, I threw the knife. It was stuck in the brick wall.

Billy heard the sound and came running. Mitchell told him I threw a knife at him. Billy didn't give me a second to explain what that fool had done to me. He stormed down, yanked the knife from the wall, and came at me furious. He lifted me in the air and body slammed me onto the floor (wham!), then grabbed me up from the floor by the shirt in the air warning me never to do anything that could kill my brother again. He said one of the younger brothers could've been coming down the stairs and gotten hit. He didn't say a word to Mitchell.

Mitchell stood behind him with a dirty smirk on his face, knowing he instigated the ordeal.

When Malree got home, Billy told her everything. She was furious. She told him to bring me downstairs. I knew she was going to whip me. Before she could, I broke loose and ran out the back door. Billy had to let me go so he wouldn't accidentally get hit. I ran through Latimer Manor as fast as I could. Billy and Mitchell chased me. Billy yelled to some friends to catch me, but I ran past them before they could react. Once they realized what was happening, they all joined the chase.

Eventually, I got tired and stopped behind some apartments to rest. As I was catching my breath, Billy came around the corner mad as ever. He grabbed one arm, put his other hand around my neck, he and Mitchell walked me a mile back home. It was embarrassing. When we got home, Malree whipped me outside in public for running away.

I felt ashamed defending myself, I was so confused. I refused to allow him to intimidate or hurt me. My big idea was to get a knife out of anger which was wrong. People's reactions made me question everything—why I even existed. I was angry about it all, I didn't like my family. I hated how I felt, but I had no other choice.

At this time, I was in fifth grade at Wardlaw Elementary. I was athletic but didn't look the part, some people didn't believe I played football. I didn't have the body yet, so people overlooked me. Everything happening in my life was psychologically devastating and shaped a pattern that followed me into my teens and adult life. The only dream I had was to be a fireman—ever since I was five. You'll see later how that dream was crushed.

I remember my fifth-grade teacher asking what our fathers did for work. I lied because I didn't know. I told the class he was a fireman. Then she gave us a survey about our personalities and how we think. When she read the results, mine said I had the personality of a minister. She said, "Phillip, you may become a preacher." I thought, *No way.* The only connection was that two of my dad's brothers were preachers, but I didn't think about what my mother told me that day until I was forced into early retirement years later.

Our mother was eventually admitted into a nursing home. We visited every Sunday until she passed. I was the last to be told. The assistant principal came to my class and brought me into the hallway. Malree was waiting, crying. She said Mom died. I felt something inside me shut down. I went numb. I didn't show emotion even as Malree hugged me.

I lost the only person who truly understood me. All I wanted was for her to get better and be proud of me. After the funeral, I returned to school and noticed my mind felt different. I focused more in class. I stopped fighting except when bullies pushed it. People heard about my fights, and since I played sports and we didn't bother anyone, nobody saw us as cowards. Billy and Mitchell wouldn't tolerate that. Losing was fine—but we had to fight back. That's how Mom and our uncles raised us.

I played sports. I had two brothers to look up to, and my younger brothers looked up to me. We all had a bond—except Mitchell. He was in his own world. Billy and I talked about it a lot, trying to understand him. Billy was in tenth grade then. Malree was in her late forties, Joseph a year younger than me, and John four years younger. We were good boys. Our grandmother never worried about where we were at night. Mitchell helped John with homework. Joe, because of his disability, was always in special classes and had chores instead of regular homework. After finishing them, he'd go outside for hours. He was the most outgoing and popular of us all—naturally strong muscles since he was a baby.

Even though he had that disease, he was the happiest guy you'd ever meet. Too strong to mess with but never fought. His condition was obvious—he couldn't walk in a straight line. Police would stop him thinking he was drunk. They eventually got to know him and even me through him. They'd tell me when they found him hanging around people who weren't good for him. Joe thought he could do everything normally, but as he got older, the disease worsened.

The summer before fifth grade was a psychological roller coaster. I played tackle football and baseball in the community. Billy and Mitchell rode me hard, telling me to stop playing scared. My confidence was growing, but I was still too skinny. Baseball fit me better. I played first base, outfield, and hit well.

One of the hardest things was watching Mom's health decline. Her suffering grew until she could barely swallow. She was moved to a nursing home. We visited her every Sunday. I loved seeing her, but she wasn't the same. One Sunday she didn't recognize us. Fear hit hard. We realized we'd never see her the same again. It showed us what Joe would eventually face too. He was the only one diagnosed, and that disease takes faith and courage to endure. Many don't make it. It's a horrible life to live through.

Every day I wondered if I had it too. I struggled to memorize things and was labeled "slow." I developed a negative outlook on myself. I thought maybe the disease was already affecting my mind. Fear controlled everything. I hated being me. It drained my confidence.

Football became something I needed. Coaches preached confidence, and they sensed I lacked it. They saw my inconsistency but couldn't understand the storm going on within me—trauma from childhood shaping my mind.

Then came the incident that changed my life forever.

# Chapter 5 — The Strike That Altered My Sight and Life

While my siblings and I were in Billy's room playing on the bed, Billy did something to John that made him scream out loud. John always did that for attention, and it usually made the adults think someone was bullying him. His fake scream brought Malree up the stairs with a broken piece of ironing cord in her hand, ready to whip us. Billy and Mitchell were too big for her to even try hitting, so she came straight toward me without asking a single question.

The moment I saw that cord, I knew I wasn't sticking around to get hit. I dodged past her as fast as I could. She swung the cord as I ran, and it landed across the back of my head and into my eye. I dropped to the floor in excruciating pain—the exposed copper wires had struck me directly in the eye. I rolled across the floor crying, covering my face with my hands and yelling, "You hit me in my eye!" I was in shock and couldn't do anything but lay there and cry.

Billy rushed over and lifted me from the floor so Malree could look at me. When she saw my eye swollen shut, fear hit everybody in the room. She sent Mitchell to get an ice pack.

Later, I went to my mother's room so she could look at my eye. She gently placed her hand over it and prayed for me. She was such a compassionate woman, and even though I knew she wanted to protect me, she was too sick to do so. Nobody realized how bad the injury was or how heavily it would weigh on my already fragile mind.

My eye stayed swollen shut for a week, and I wore shades every day to hide it. Two weeks after the swelling went down, we were all sitting at the table eating dinner when my uncle Joe looked at me and said, "Boy, what's that in your eye?" The second he said it, everybody stared at me, and fear took over. As Malree leaned in to look, her whole expression changed. That scared me even more.

I ran to the bathroom to check. When I looked in the mirror, I saw a tiny gray dot in my eye. After two weeks of swelling—now *this*? My heart ached. I thought it was something that could never be fixed. When I came back to the table, Uncle Joe asked what happened. I didn't know what to say, so Billy told him that Malree accidentally hit me in the eye. Uncle Joe said, "You need to take that boy to the doctor." Then he asked if I could still see. I said yes, even though I was terrified.

The next week, Malree made an appointment with an ophthalmologist. I was eleven. Before going, she sat me down and told me not to tell the doctor the truth about what happened or we'd be separated and placed in a boys' home by DSS. I didn't want that. I hated going to the Welfare Department already. One of my older siblings always had to miss school to accompany her for the monthly evaluations, and it embarrassed them. They eventually refused to go and told her to take me instead since I was old enough. I didn't mind skipping school—school wasn't my favorite place—but I understood why they didn't want to go.

Before the appointment, Billy and Mitchell pulled me aside and told me I had to lie to the doctor. If I told the truth, they said, Malree could go to jail for child abuse and we'd all end up in foster care. They were worried I might still be angry at her—and I was—but I couldn't bring myself to use that against her. Even though the injury changed my life, I didn't want to hurt her back. I told them I'd say it happened while playing baseball.

At the appointment, the doctor asked what happened and why we hadn't come sooner. I told him I got hit in the eye with a baseball.

Malree added that the swelling had hidden the issue. The doctor said I might have been too young to notice the change in my vision at first. After examining me, he told me to stop playing baseball, he warned I would start getting severe migraine headaches, and said I'd need surgery when I turned sixteen.

Hearing that scared me to my core. How did I endure?

I started keeping that eye halfway closed so people wouldn't notice the cataract, which grew bigger as time passed. I became painfully self-conscious about my appearance and dealt with headaches constantly. I didn't inform my coaches what was going on because I didn't understand it myself. The migraine headaches happened during football practice which caused me to be less aggressive.

Another situation with Malree also changed my life: music.

In fifth grade, we had to learn an instrument to join the band the next year. The band instructor sent home a notice saying I needed a snare drum kit. Playing drums was my gift, I played by ear—I could feel rhythm in everything. Every Saturday, we'd go downtown. The Woolworth department store had a snare drum kit on display for seventy-five dollars. I'd tap on it every time we went to the store until Malree told me to stop because she was afraid I'd damage it. They also sold a toy drum set in a box, which I secretly dreamed of getting for Christmas.

When I showed her the notice from school, she said she didn't have the money but would get a drum. I told her exactly where the snare drum was. She said she'd get it the following week.

That next week, I watched out the window every ten minutes waiting for her. When I finally saw her walking toward the apartment carrying a big box, I was so disappointed. It was the *toy* drum set—the one in the box. I stood there devastated. How did she think I could take a toy drum to school? I didn't understand then that she simply couldn't afford the real one. My brothers were excited and tore open the box to set it up, but I couldn't join the school band. Playing football saved me.

One of my neighbors rode the bus with a real snare drum case. Seeing him crushed me inside. If I had known back then how to express what I felt, I wouldn't have carried that disappointment for many years. But later in life, reflecting on it helped me heal.

At the time, though, I didn't recognize my own depression. My world felt like it was falling apart—my eyesight altered, migraines, no band, no baseball, and a toy drum reminding me of what I couldn't have. That's when my whole "shadow program" began forming.

In the middle of fifth grade, the assistant principal pulled me from class. Malree stood in the hallway and told me my mother had passed away. I was sad, but I didn't cry—I felt empty. She hugged me, crying, but I didn't hug her back. It didn't feel genuine after everything that happened. Her love had always come through discipline and providing, not open affection.

When I returned to school after the funeral, I felt different—like a part of me was gone. I pushed the feelings aside and focused on sports, even though I lacked confidence in myself. Later, we received a letter about my placement for junior high. My brothers opened it and saw one of the classes was in the "special ed trailer." I just wanted out of there. I had to work harder than everyone else because of being dyslexic, but I didn't know that at the time. I wouldn't learn the truth until many years later.

Finding out our bloodline was Cherokee, Choctaw, and connected to the Moorish Americans helped me understand my identity on a conscious level, I wasn't aware of who I am. As a child through adolescence into part of adult life , I couldn't accept myself. I wanted to be like everyone around me—especially my brothers, who all seemed to have a mental edge I didn't. I became quiet and reserved. I still played sports, but I didn't hang out with teammates. I stayed home or spent time with Buck (Floyd)

I never felt comfortable playing basketball, therefore I didn't play my sophomore year despite Mitchell's encouragement. He saw me play my best game and wanted me to continue. When my junior year came and basketball season started, he pushed me again to join. I told him I didn't want to be on the team anymore—I was going to focus on football.

# Chapter 6 — The Decision That Saved My Life for a Divine Purpose

Deciding not to play basketball that year may have saved my life. I followed my intuition and stayed off the team. Our school played a game at a local school not far from where me and some team mates lived. After the game, a car filled with players from my neighborhood was involved in a serious accident in front of the school. One person was paralyzed from the neck down. The others had broken legs and arms.

When I heard the news the next morning, I walked up and down the backyard thinking about how close I came to being in that car. I was battling stress at the time, but I was grateful I wasn't on that team. I felt like I had a spiritual gift—like, for once, I made the right decision for myself. Deep down, I knew I'd been spared for a divine purpose. I walked the yard thinking about God and how easily I could've been with those guys, we grew up together. I felt the same protective love I'd felt years earlier when that crazy man chased me under a house with a knife. He got within three feet of me before suddenly turning away.

I believed God had a purpose for my life. Still, I didn't realize that rejecting myself—because of my memory struggles and self-doubt—meant I was also rejecting Emmanuel, God within me. I couldn't stay angry. I was soft-spoken, but I wasn't afraid of people; I was afraid of myself. I showed compassion and forgiveness toward my grandmother because something in me chose to. I couldn't disrespect her.

Because I was quiet, I had to stand up to bullies, and once they learned I would fight, it was too late for them. People who were aggressive or controlling assumed I was weak—a pushover or incompetent. I didn't deal with people like that then, and I still don't. I wouldn't engage in conversation with them, so they labeled me weird or crazy. I couldn't stand being around people who knowingly hurt others. I wasn't at peace around them. I wanted peace of mind, so I stayed to myself—an introvert tired of navigating deceptive, dishonest, narcissistic people.

One positive thing about being an introvert was that I learned who people really were. I let them think I was stupid. Quiet people were stereotyped as dangerous, so folks kept their distance. I let people believe they could take advantage of me so I could see their true nature. A lot of them were deceitful and traitorous. That energy followed me for years until I finally broke the pattern by not associating with those kinds of people.

I had to break the chains that enslaved my mind. I took responsibility and started freeing myself from other people's opinions. I had to learn to love myself beyond the thoughts created by the world around me. I thought the problem was within me, but it wasn't.

People knew I was harmless unless provoked. Coaches and teachers liked me, though some were frustrated because I didn't hang out with the team and they couldn't motivate me to push beyond my athletic ability. They always talked about having that "mental edge," and that's where I struggled. They liked me enough to want to see me succeed, I was too inconsistent.

By seventh grade, I had to learn how to like myself. My sports performance was inconsistent, and I focused on it because my older brothers were strong football players. I played Line Backer and compared to Billy's hard nose play, we played the same position. When my seventh-grade schedule arrived in the mail, Billy and Mitchell opened it and saw that one of my classes was in a trailer—the Special Ed class. They bullied me for being quiet and unsure of myself. I had to fight through that every day because I knew I could do better. I felt pressure to improve and change, but I couldn't figure myself out.

I was older now, my mother was gone, and I feared dying the same way she did. Every morning, I checked my hands and legs for tremors. I'd stare at my hands during class because I was so nervous, I was always nervous and unsure.

I knew I didn't belong in that classroom, but I couldn't figure out how to read faster or memorize things. My mind wandered every time I tried to study. I'd focus on a sentence, then drift off trying to understand it. I didn't believe in myself, and no one was there to help me understand me. Instead of going to the gym or hanging out with friends during school, I looked for quiet places to study because studying took me longer.

Still, I didn't like school, and I didn't like being myself. I couldn't wait to graduate. I just had to work harder.

My brothers and I stayed out of major trouble. People didn't know me the way they knew my brothers because I didn't hang around the neighborhood. I spent most of my time in my room listening to music, playing 45s and albums, and lifting Billy's weights. I stayed to myself because I felt I didn't fit in.

I hung out with a few close friends—Floyd Dowling (Buck), Samuel Stewart (West), Stephon Byrd, and Darnell Scott—until we graduated. One of the few romantic relationships I had in high school was with Buck's sister, Lois, who was embarrassed to let people know we were talking. Back then, I wasn't attractive to most girls because I wasn't vocal or charismatic, even though I was outgoing in sports. I wasn't considered a ladies' man; the pretty girls called me ugly. I was the least known of my family. I dated a cheerleader from Eau Claire High School named Shirley Salter for a year before dating one Floyd Sisters, Deloris

One day, while walking home, a woman named Mrs. Bush stopped me. She knew all my brothers except me—Billy was friends with her son June—but she didn't know me because I was too quiet. She scolded me for walking by without speaking. She thought I was being disrespectful. After I apologized, she realized I was a good person. Once people got to know me, they liked me—unless they were mean, disrespectful or evil.

I was peaceful—so peaceful that when I went to a drug dealer's house to buy marijuana, he thought I was an undercover cop. Years later, we both were members of the same church, he told me he used to follow me with a .38 pistol and a shotgun just to make sure. His name was the late John "Blob" Penny, a talented athlete. We became close friends twelve years later when I accepted Christ and joined the church he was a member of. I didn't know he attended until we talked after service and he told me that story. John had the highest Bible IQ of anyone I knew. As we grew in ministry together, I wanted to be like him. Looking back, I realized I was repeating the same pattern I'd had since childhood—struggling to accept myself.

Within the next two years, my family dynamic began to change. I focused more on finishing school and becoming a fireman—my dream job. I didn't think about any other career. I was always respectful to Malree but never vocal toward adults. My brothers and I knew we had to be responsible for ourselves, and the older brothers would handle us if we weren't. We were independent because Malree was getting older—she was in her mid-fifties—and we had to take care of ourselves. When we had concerns, we voiced them, and it was understood.

Malree slowed down from working and stayed home cooking for us every day. She didn't go to church as much, but the late Mother Lloyd and the late Bishop A.C. Jackson and his wife from Bible Way Church of Atlas Road visited her often. I thought she wasn't feeling well, but I ignored my intuition. Something wasn't right. She wanted to teach me how to cook because all her recipes were in her mind. I told her cooking was for girls and I didn't have time, but she still showed me how to make sweet potato pies.

She wanted to teach me because she was getting weaker, but she didn't tell us why, somehow I was the person she was turning to, I started feeling important.

I heard rumors that people encouraged my brother Joe to dance even though he had a condition that caused him to shake uncontrollably. They laughed and called him "Shaky Box." Some people labeled our family as crazy. Joe was strong and outgoing. People saw him lifting weights and wrestling, although I rarely saw it because he went places I didn't. Folks knew me only as one of the Pittman brothers. Joe had good people who looked out for him.

Meanwhile, home life with Mitchell grew more unbearable. Mitchell verbally abused Malree every day. He destroyed her plants and broke her decorations, calling them worthless. He was mean. Billy and I tried talking to him about his disrespect, but he refused to claim her as our grandmother because of what he believed she did to our mother. He carried anger and bitterness within himself. He was too big to confront when he was like that, there was no convincing him otherwise.

But in public—especially at school—it was a different story. The girls found out I was his brother and asked me to give him their numbers or see if he had a girlfriend. That angered me, but I passed the notes anyway. Eventually I realized all I had to do was tell them how mean he was, and it would stop.

I learned a lot about women during that time—mostly what I didn't want to be a part of.

Living with Mitchell was hell, but it didn't stop me from improving myself. We thought his behavior was normal because we were used to it, but it wasn't. Malree knew that. Billy told me she said Mitchell had "two faces." She saw evil in him and believed he wouldn't function well in the world, she was correct.

The truth was he was bipolar. In many homes, that disorder becomes a learned pattern. Children see the aggressive person gain control by manipulating others' emotions. The problem is that behavior carries into adult life and careers. That's how we end up with highly educated, successful people whose mental instability and lack of moral grounding destroy their common sense making it difficult to work with.

# Chapter 7 — The Salvation and Transformation of Billy

My oldest brother Billy graduated from Columbia High School with the class of 1976. After that, he enrolled at Midlands Technical College, Columbia, S.C. Billy stayed active, was in a relationship, and worked a summer job maintaining the Latimer Manor social building and grounds before starting school. Once he stopped working, they hired me to take over his job.

Back then, I didn't like myself much, so Billy was my idol. When people saw me for the first time, they'd say, "That boy looks just like Billy Pittman." I never understood it. I thought I was ugly. I wanted to be like Billy so badly that I even asked for one of his old T-shirts. He laughed and handed it to me. It was red and white, fit my new muscles, and on the back was a red devil holding a pitchfork with the words: **"Live it up—we're all going to hell anyway."**

I wore that shirt to the Winn-Dixie grocery store one day. As I was leaving, a man yelled for me to stop. He walked up, leaned in, and said, "Son, you need to take that shirt off. The devil is a liar—everybody ain't going to hell." I said, "Yes sir," because I had a bad feeling he was a Pastor, (lol). When I got home, I gave Billy the shirt back and told him what happened. Billy laughed and said, "Yeah, he is a Pastor—we're friends." I was pissed. He set me up for that one.

The summer of 1977 changed everything for us—especially Billy. Suddenly, his life shifted. He broke up with his girlfriend, and his best friend ended up dating her. He quit the job at the office and told me to work in his place. Then he fell into a deep depression. I had never seen him like that. Something was seriously wrong.

One evening I came home from hanging out with Buck and found Malree at the table crying. I asked what happened, and she lifted her head and said, Billy was in the hospital. The news startled me, I was in shock. Billy tried to kill himself by eating rat poison. Malree rushed him to the ER, and they saved his life. He stayed in the hospital for two days for evaluation.

When he came home, he was different—slouched over, walking slow, his hands curled inward, his voice dragging. Malree helped care for him because she knew what pushed him over the edge: Billy found out he had the same disease our mother and Joe had been diagnosed with, and he didn't want to face that kind of suffering.

I couldn't imagine what Malree felt—watching one child recover while knowing another was declining.

In her mind, she saw something none of us were ready for: I might need to become head of the household. Mitchell was the second oldest, but she would never choose him for anything. He challenged everyone, hated correction, and carried bitterness like it was his birthright. When someone is mentally unstable, love from others feels like an attack. Mitchell wasn't someone you wanted around when you were sick.

Mitchell had "celebrity" status in the family, while I stayed quiet and observant. I promised myself I would never start a family with someone mentally unstable. I refused to follow the patterns I saw in him. Every family deals with mental illness differently—sometimes it's diagnosed, most times it's ignored and passed off as "just how they are."

The following year, Billy was recovering, though slowly. Around 1978, I was sixteen, our dad called from Jersey City and invited me to spend the summer with him. I took the Greyhound bus there. Dad worked during the day, therefore I stayed alone in the apartment. He told me not to let anyone in and explained where I should and shouldn't go. He kept all kinds of liquor, and while he was at work, I'd go to the park to train for football season, grab lunch, then return to the apartment.

I saw plenty of beautiful girls that summer, but I stayed away. I had no intention of becoming a teenage father. After eating, I'd head back to the apartment, drink liquor, listen to music, or watch TV.

Then Dad threw me into the fire—he got me a job at the same plant where he worked: Crown, Cork & Seal, a soda can company in Jersey City, New Jersey. He was an engineer there. I worked the second shift, sleeping during the day. I was young and strong, but the job was brutal. I had to lift heavy wooden planks onto a conveyor belt and stack seven layers of cans with cardboard between each one. I had to stay ahead of the machine so the engineer didn't have to stop it. If the machine stopped, a supervisor would get right in your face. One night I was so tired and not feeling well the supervisor threatened to tell my dad I was getting behind.

The warehouse was huge and had no air conditioning. It felt like working in hell. Some nights I woke up sweating from nightmares. But the pay was good. Another football player who worked there used to sit on the roof smoking weed, staring out at the George Washington Bridge and the New York City skyline. It was beautiful—lights for miles.

On weekends my aunt and her friends took me to New York dance clubs. They had a van that felt like a living room on wheels, music blasting as we drove through the city. Things were going so well that Dad asked me to move there permanently. He said I had a good job and he'd take care of the rest.

I told him I loved visiting, but city life wasn't for me. I wanted my senior year of football. I didn't want to leave my family.

While I was gone, Billy took months to recover from the rat poison. He started lifting weights and eventually looked physically normal again, but mentally he still wasn't himself. One winter he shaved his head bald. One morning, while we were loading onto the school bus, Billy came outside in a sweatsuit. The bus couldn't leave because he stood in front of it in a three-point stance like he was about to play football. Mitchell tried to get him inside, but Billy refused. I stayed on the bus—I didn't want trouble. Eventually, Malree and a neighbor convinced him to go home.

After about a year, Billy made a full transformation. Some of his friends were members of the Progressive Church of Our Lord Jesus Christ on Barhamsville Rd. in Columbia, S.C., Billy accepted Jesus as his Lord and Savior and joined that church. The members knew our mother and how faithful she'd been, even though she was a member of a different church.

Billy's life changed. His peace and joy returned. I felt it. He gave me love and respect, and I returned it. Mitchell loved us too, but sometimes he lacked respect, which made his love feel flawed. There are levels to love depending on a person's consciousness. Love penetrates everything—people either accept it or reject it based on their emotional maturity. We had a deep inner love I didn't understand then. It was so strong we didn't need words.

But I didn't believe in myself enough to accept that same love for me. I watched love heal Billy when he finally accepted his life and walked the path he was called to follow. His sorrow turned into joy. I remember feeling happy because God was real to us—it was more than religion. It was something within, something only church folks understood back then, something our grandmother and mother instilled in us.

They saw it in me too—once I got past my childhood struggles—but I couldn't see it in myself yet.

During this time, I was between fifteen and eighteen, weighing between 160-185 pounds and I started excelling athletically. When I told Mitchell I was trying out for the junior high track team, he didn't think I could make it. He discouraged me because I was skinny, even though I was building muscle. The other guys were bigger, but I made the team—and that shocked him.

I qualified for the long jump  but strained my right quadriceps doing it. Coach Crosby got frustrated because I kept reacting to the pain while he was treating my injury with Icy Hot. Ironically, that was my best jump ever. Mitchell didn't realize how badly I was injured. I wouldn't learn the truth until thirty years later when I developed sciatica and went to a chiropractor. X-rays showed my right hip had been off balance since birth. When I told him I'd played football, he explained that years of pressure on that side caused constant inflammation as I aged. I had strained muscles on that side my whole life without knowing why.

Some coaches thought I was mentally weak. Really, I just didn't know how to explain my pain. If I complained, I was labeled undisciplined. I didn't know how to compensate for the issue because nobody knew about my hip alignment. I caused myself problems simply by not understanding my body. Worst of all, I believed the negative things people said. Some of my coaches didn't believe in me, they said Billy was tougher, they compared me to him because we were similar in size but I was smaller.

But within me there was a great love holding me together—wrapped around my mind like a chain I couldn't break. People mistook it for weakness, and for years, so did I.

Billy's transformation was a miracle. We lived in harmony—even Mitchell.

But 1978 changed everything.

**Malree passed away from complications of breast cancer.**

She'd noticed a lump in her breast but waited too long to have it examined out of fear we'd end up in foster care or separated among relatives. She grew so weak she couldn't argue with Mitchell anymore, and he didn't realize she was sick until she could barely function. When he finally understood, he changed because she wasn't a challenge any more.

I worked part-time after school in the dietary department at a local Hospital, where Malree was hospitalized. I visited her every day. I was terrified she'd die. Fear gripped me, but I had to be strong.

As her illness progressed, we had to stick together. I was the only one with a real job. Billy and Joe were disabled received SSI from Social Service. Mitchell received several football scholarship offers—Wofford College, South Carolina State, and others which lifted Malree's spirits.

When she came home after surgery, we had to feed and nurse her. They removed her right breast and lymph nodes from her armpit, leaving a wound that couldn't fully heal. The incision was so severe that Billy and Mitchell couldn't stomach cleaning the area. They called me into Billy's room and told me they couldn't do it and Malree asked for me to take care of her, therefore I cleaned and dressed her wound every day until she returned to the hospital for the final time. She was dying when they discharged her initially. She knew she wouldn't survive the surgery.

Caring for her felt like something I was meant to do. The wound didn't bother me—knowing she couldn't live with it did. She thanked me for helping her and said she needed to return to the hospital. She died a week later.

Afterward, we held a brother's meeting to figure out how to survive without her. We knew Mitchell would be going away to college. He chose Wofford on a full football scholarship and played for three years before joining the Army.

# Chapter 8 — The Passing of Malree Placed Me as Head of Household at Sixteen

We received a letter from the Housing Authority addressed to *me*, asking for a meeting with Mr. Herbert Walker, the director of Housing Authority. All of us read it, wondering why they wanted *me* instead of Billy or Mitchell. Joe and John were too young. I was sixteen—and terrified.

Mr. Walker remembered Billy and me from working at the Latimer Manor community center. He told me my grandmother, Malree, had spoken with him about her illness, and that she expected to die. She requested that I be named head of household so I could care for my brothers.

He said our family had always been respectful and never caused trouble, so he wanted to help. But I was too young to legally be on the lease, and Billy couldn't be listed because of his past mental condition—though he didn't know Billy had long since recovered. Mitchell wasn't an option because he'd be leaving for college, and Malree didn't trust his judgment.

Mr. Walker asked when I'd turn seventeen. I told him June 18th, the following summer. He said, "Because you'll be seventeen soon, I'll put seventeen on the application. We'll make it work." He warned that I had to stay responsible for myself and my brothers, then went over the guidelines we needed to follow.

When I came home, everyone was waiting. I told them the news—**we didn't have to move.** We celebrated. We were young, independent, and, for the most part, we respected each other.

With Mitchell gone, it was on me to keep peace at home. Joe and John were coming in too late on school nights. Billy stayed active in church and helped John with homework. Joe, though, wandered everywhere. He hung around people who didn't have his best interests at heart. He was joyful and outgoing—but vulnerable.

Joe attended W.J. Keenan High School because they had the special classes he needed. Many of his friends lived in another neighborhood, so he walked there regularly. One evening Billy told me Joe smelled like alcohol and warned that people might be taking advantage of him. Joe wouldn't listen—he thought he was just having fun.

Joe graduated high school in 1981. Without school keeping him busy, we had to get him into programs. One night I waited for Joe and John to come home and laid down new rules about curfews. They knew better than to argue with me.

Mitchell visited on weekends to spend time with John, who was a very good football player for Columbia High School; he graduated in 1984.

But Joe worried me the most. I had to make him understand people were using him. I explained how some folks pushed him to drink or smoke just for their own entertainment. While I prayed on what to do, Emmanuel (God with us) opened my mind. I reminded Joe about the power that saved Billy. I told him we had to protect each other. I couldn't defend him if he kept hanging around the wrong crowd.

I talked about our mother, about God's love for her, about how God healed Billy. Then I did something simple—but powerful. I handed Joe a Bible and one of his old schoolbooks and asked him to read from both. He read the Bible verse clearly but couldn't read a single sentence from the schoolbook.

I was stunned. I called Billy in to see it, and we both stood there amazed.

I told Joe he needed to join the church with Billy—that Jesus would protect him and give him a better life. The next time Billy went to church, Joe went too and accepted Christ.

After that, the two of them were inseparable. Their faith bonded them so strongly that girls stopped coming to our apartment to visit me—nobody wanted to test Billy's newfound devotion to God.

What struck me most was that **I had led Joe to Christ without stepping foot in church myself.** There was something inside me that connected to God inwardly, even though I couldn't explain it. I felt His presence constantly.

Billy and Joe stayed true to their faith. Billy moved into an apartment next to the church, and Joe moved in with him in 1983. John and I lived together for a year after he graduated. I couldn't wait to finish high school myself. I had enough credits to graduate early, but chose to stay for my senior year. I only needed one class—English—so I had half-days.

From 1981 to 1984, I worked part-time in the dietary department at a local hospital. During that time, I wrote comedy plays, recruited volunteer actors, and performed them in talent shows. Caroline Montgomery and I co-wrote my first play, **"Little Wolfie Is Coming Home,"** introducing today's Da Wolf character wearing a werewolf mask. I wrote two more successful plays for the hospital's annual employee shows. I bought my first drum set, formed a band, and we performed Michael Jackson's **"Billie Jean."**

Writing became a gift I discovered after countless hours alone in my room listening to music, drinking Schlitz Malt Liquor Bull, and watching cable TV. I needed something to keep my mind entertained. I smoked my first joint at sixteen with Buck. We were teenage boys stealing our older brothers' ID's, and porn magazines.

I didn't go to many parties or clubs—I saw too many people doing dirty things behind each other's backs. I walked everywhere or took the bus. Most of my friends had cars except Stephon Byrd. The rest would drive past me on the road without stopping, they didn't give me a ride but I was used to being treated in that fashion.

I graduated high school in 1980 at seventeen and enrolled in Midlands Technical College's carpentry program, graduating in 1982. I didn't pursue carpentry immediately because I didn't know who to contact, and the hospital job felt steady. After graduating, I was offered a full-time position in the dietary department and took it. I worked a year in the pot sink before applying for a transporter position in the main lab.

I'd always wanted to be a fireman. I even worked for the fire department at fifteen, painting hydrants across the City of Columbia, which made me want it even more. I applied to the City of Columbia Fire Department, got an interview, but wasn't hired the first time at age nineteen. I planned to try again.

When Billy and Joe were stable, we brothers talked about the military. Billy thought it'd be a good opportunity for all of us if I were stationed nearby. A recruiter said the Army would be best for what we needed. I didn't want the Army—I wanted the Air Force.

I took the Air Force test but didn't score high enough. Twenty minutes later, a high-ranking Army officer came in and called my name and another guy's. I said, "Sir, I took the Air Force test," but he told me I didn't score high enough. Without explaining anything, he stood between us and took pictures. The other guy and I asked why. He said, "We can't tell you now."

It was bittersweet. I didn't want the Army, but the process swept me up anyway.

The final step was the eye exam. When they called me up, I couldn't read the right side clearly. The officer said I'd done well on the written exam, but I had to pass the eye test to join.

# Chapter 9 — The Transformation into Adult Life Became Spiritually Frustrating at Work

Despite the challenges I faced at work, home life stayed stable. Everyone was happy. Billy was proud to have Joe in church with him. They never wavered in their faith—they were committed to growing in the Holiness tradition. John had a job and moved into an apartment in West Columbia, South Carolina. He seemed to be doing well, and our schedules kept us from seeing much of each other.

My personality has always been kind, respectful, and considerate. I was well liked by the lab director, the late Ron Noble—the man who hired me—and by the late A.J. Cox, supervisor of Phlebotomy. Word spread about how I was being disrespected openly in the department office by an administrator. Because of that, I gained friends who'd had similar experiences. People realized I wasn't ignorant and that my personality was genuine. Before long, I became a topic of discussion throughout the lab. Folks talked to me about what they heard, but I stayed wise and quiet. Over time, they realized I understood more than they gave me credit for.

One day, A.J. walked into the blood-drawing station while I was reading a small Bible. He asked if I'd be interested in becoming a phlebotomist. He'd heard about what I was dealing with in the office and told me I didn't deserve that kind of disrespect because of my personality which wasn't a problem with him. I told him I was interested but needed to know the steps. I already knew how to draw blood—I watched it every day. A.J. believed in me. He told me I could take the class and pass. I felt excited. It was a way out of that work environment.

During that time, I held all my frustrations inside. In high school, sports helped me release stress. As an adult, I had no outlet and no mental support. I was twenty two, a mature adult but still unsure of myself because of how others judged me. I thought about being unkind to people who were unkind to me, but I didn't want to lose myself. Something within me kept pulling me toward goodness, even while I was fighting it. I didn't know how to fix myself. I was introverted, and people who didn't know me assumed I was arrogant.

I kept certain thoughts to myself because I didn't want to become hard or bitter. I finally accepted that I was in the "real world" and didn't quite fit into it. I was becoming a man who needed discipline. Word got back to me that some people thought I was too dumb to get a job outside the main office. I refused to gossip. My personal life was fine, but I knew I could be more—I just didn't know how. My biggest battle wasn't with people; it was with myself. I felt chained up inside, without freedom. The shadow work I learned later in life would've helped me back then.

Every morning on my walk to work, I passed an attractive young woman waiting for the bus. We exchanged greetings. After about a month, I asked what time she gets home, and she invited me to visit her apartment. She seemed nice as we talked on the walk to my apartment. She didn't drink or smoke and told me she was a Christian—which puzzled me later when she ended up locked in my room with me. I didn't make a move on her, thinking she might be a respectable woman. She later invited me to her church—a new, non-denominational ministry headquartered in Tennessee. Their local meetings were held in the Latimer Manor social room. I felt nervous walking in. About twenty people were there at the time.

As soon as I sat down, the late Mr. John Penny came up and hugged me with excitement. He and his wife Melissa had been members there for a year. I was shocked and happy to see John saved. He had been a well-known drug dealer I used to buy from, but now he was a deacon—a "Thug for Jesus," as he called himself. The Pennys were exactly the encouragement I needed.

The pastor's message that day was the same scripture I'd read at work the day before. I had been reading the Bible often because I was searching for a change within myself. I felt drawn to it—almost called. I needed peace of mind. I kept silent about my responsibilities and personal life at work, so none of my coworkers knew what I was carrying.

After that first visit, John introduced me to the pastor, who lit up when he heard about our past friendship and his connection to my family—especially my grandmother. He invited me back and said he wanted me involved in the ministry alongside Brother Penny, which intrigued me.

Joining that church felt like a chance to finally live by God's truth. I didn't know enough truth about myself to keep living in confusion and rejection. I felt rejected because of who people thought I was supposed to be. Feeling God's unconditional love working in my mind was powerful, even though I didn't fully understand the relationship yet. I needed to shift my focus from people to myself. Fear had gripped my confidence for too long. My thoughts had no balance, and every day felt like a battle. Life is a battle already won, but we still have to walk through it. Up to this point, my blueprint came from not accepting myself—and wanting to be smart like John Penny, who had an incredible ability to quote scripture, remember chapter and verse, and actually live it.

Reading the Bible felt like a calling. But I struggled with surrendering to Christ because I felt lost inside, like something was missing. I wondered how I could find happiness within and what joining a church would really mean. Meanwhile, things at work grew worse. Some people intentionally made the job miserable. I didn't want to grow bitter or vengeful, but I fought that urge daily. I wanted out of the lab. Sitting in the office for eight hours doing nothing—only to have my conversations twisted against me—was unbearable. People twisted my words even though I avoided drama.

My only solution was to limit communication with those types unless necessary—and always keep it professional. As more people in the lab got to know me, they saw I had spiritual wisdom and was pleasant to talk to. Yet rumors from the main office painted me as incapable of learning anything, as incompetent. The truth was simple: I didn't want to learn from people who looked down on me. I didn't care what they said—until I got tired of it. People warned me to watch my back. That kind of environment was new to me. I wanted to fight back, but no one had my back, and I didn't want to lose my job. People depended on me.

One morning, when I walked into the office, they were holding a meeting. The lead person pointed at me and said, "I don't want to see you this morning. Go sit in the drawing area." I turned around and headed to my favorite place—where the patients and phlebotomists were happy to see me. Honestly, it made my day.

As I sat in the drawing area, I asked A.J. if I could become a phlebotomist since I'd practically been training already. He was thrilled. I asked if he believed I could succeed. He said yes—but I needed certification. He gave me everything I needed to sign up. I felt anxious and excited. School scared me because of my memory issues, but I had no choice. When I told the office I was going to phlebotomy school, they were shocked. Some didn't believe I'd pass. They didn't know me at all.

After football season, Mitchell came home on weekends. I didn't see him or John much because of work and school. He helped John move into his apartment in West Columbia. A year later, Mitchell told me John had been diagnosed with the disease. I was devastated. Suddenly his distance made sense. He was still working but stayed hidden so people wouldn't see the physical changes. Hearing his diagnosis reminded me of what our family doctor told my mother—that three or four of us would have the same disease. I was terrified daily, thinking I would be next. I couldn't imagine how John felt dealing with that alone, his girlfriend whom he married was never there when I visited.

Once I finished the phlebotomy course, I visited John twice a week. I questioned why he moved so far, but he never answered. Mitchell later told me his girlfriend's mother lived nearby which is why John was always alone and in the dark when I visited. My thoughts grew heavier, pushing me closer to giving my life to Christ. I went to church alone one evening. As I listened to the message, I knew it was my night. I was nervous about going up front, afraid I'd say something wrong. But I didn't care anymore. Something deep within—something no woman, no money, no material thing could offer—was calling me. I had to change my life, even if I didn't know how.

That evening was exciting and unforgettable.

# Chapter 10 – My Transition into Christian Life Added Many Challenges

That church was exactly where I was meant to be during that season of my life. When I gave my life to Emmanuel (God with us), the whole congregation rejoiced. The pastor knew about John and my past friendship, and everyone knew me as a quiet, respectful young man. As I matured spiritually, I became deeply involved in church activities—choir rehearsal, prayer meetings, anything I could help with. I even tried singing, but I couldn't carry a tune. I sang so low nobody could hear me. I felt so uncomfortable that I asked the pastor if they needed a drummer instead, since I already owned a drum set. They did—so I started playing drums with the choir.

I joined the prison ministry, and the pastor paired John Penny and me together to visit different neighborhoods. People everywhere recognized John and listened when he spoke. It was powerful watching him testify about Jesus Christ. He never tried to convince people to "get

Churchie." He taught them to love the Lord and become the living word. He told me to study the Bible and speak it into existence with faith and love because the word is alive—and so is Jesus' love for people.

He also showed me how the word becomes prophetic when applied correctly. As we grew together, people noticed we had similar gifts, or anointing. About a year later, John was ordained as the church Prophet, and I was ordained a Deacon. I connected with that kind of love naturally. We shared a passion for life and for people. I was sincere about my transformation. It wasn't magic—my problems didn't disappear just because I had a new consciousness. But that consciousness created a better man within me. I didn't have to fight myself alone anymore, though I still had to learn how to love myself.

Within six months to a year—around age twenty-three—I was ordained first as an usher and then as a deacon. The Penny family, a few other members, and I started holding Bible studies at a boarding house. Since I was single, the pastor trusted me to escort single women home after church. We were involved in church activities five days a week. As my faith grew, I matured as a person. Still, certain qualities had always been in me—pure love, peace, spiritual wisdom—because I kept searching for answers to my broken nature. My nature became more like John's because I thought he had the qualities I lacked. He was free to be himself with confidence.

I thought becoming a Christian would heal me from myself. Instead, it healed me from the mindset of the world—not from my own inner battles. The nature of this world is negative dominance, and I didn't understand that until much later in life. The mindset I have now didn't develop overnight, but the shift began immediately. I could finally focus on something real, even if I couldn't see it except through proper actions guided by principles like love, joy, peace, courage, freedom, and truth. Along the way, I had to learn things beyond traditional Bible teaching. We saw people living righteous lives without looking or acting "religious"—just normal. People used religion as a weapon.

Even though I was developing Christ consciousness and those emotional voids were being filled, something still felt missing. It felt like longing—a deep desire. I had a passion for spiritual truth, but nowhere to turn except staying busy at church. I met many false teachers who wanted prosperity more than God's word. Some pastors were jealous, arrogant, deceitful, and self-centered. They cared more about attention than souls, which confused me at first. Souls are the true value of every person. I was trying to find that same value in myself while watching religious leaders burn out and lose balance. I wanted something real—something that reflected the scripture:

**Matthew 7:7 — "Ask, and it will be given to you; seek, and you will find; knock, and it will be opened to you."**

As my spirit cried out, the spirit of Yeshua guided my decisions. I eventually made a major choice to return home from New Jersey because of my love for my family. Our dad wasn't there to help us survive. As you continue reading, you'll see that consciousness is the key to breaking chains of fear—including the mistakes we make because of our human nature. I struggled with decision-making because I didn't trust myself. Being dyslexic—and not knowing it—gave me horrible feelings about my abilities, but those feelings no longer controlled me.

As a single man, the church leaders trusted me to walk the ladies home through different neighborhoods. One of those members was Josie Washington. She had two children—Cornelius, eight, and Willisha (Lisa), two. Walking together after church helped us become friends, or so I thought. The other members who usually walked with us slowly drifted away, leaving Josie and me alone. She took her children to her mother's home during the week for childcare since it was far from the church. I helped her with this for about a year. I was known as a good man at church, at work, and at home.

Christian life gave me new boldness. It wouldn't let me accept disrespect at work anymore. One day I called a meeting with an office leader after being treated like an outcast for too long. People talked behind my back, and my evaluations were unfair, which kept me from receiving the raise I earned to care for my family. I had proof—someone asked me about my evaluation, which should've been confidential.

When I confronted the office leader about her treatment, quoting scripture to support my stand, she denied everything and laughed at me. Her reaction only confirmed what I already knew. I suggested bringing in each employee one by one, and she was confident they would side with her. As they came in, she explained the meeting. They all laughed and denied any mistreatment. I called them liars to their faces and used scripture to expose their behavior. They saw the change in me. I stood alone, but I wasn't shaken. Scripture had already warned

Around that time, I had two dreams with the same message. In one, I was alone in a deep hole filled with snakes—so many I couldn't see the ground. They struck my legs, and I felt the stings, but I wasn't poisoned. I was afraid but unharmed. I didn't understand those dreams, just like I didn't understand the strange visions I had as a child. I longed for answers but kept it all inside.

But there was one dream I did understand. About a month after I had it, I walked Josie and her children home. They had grown close to me. After church one day, I was cleaning the women's restroom when I overheard John Penny and the pastor talking about me. John said I was faithful and genuinely loved the Lord. The pastor agreed and said none of the church sisters had ever complained about me. He believed I wasn't in church looking for a woman, but was truly a godly brother. Then John suggested ordaining me as a deacon. The pastor agreed to put me on trial without telling me. John added, "He's already doing the work." Hearing that made me feel good. I didn't say a word, but it meant a lot that they accepted me just as I was. The pastor understood that my introverted personality wasn't a weakness.

By the time I walked to the men's restroom, John and the pastor were gone. As I cleaned, I heard women laughing. They were talking excitedly, and I heard Josie's name. She told them she'd had a dream that made them all excited. It sounded like she had a crush on someone. I didn't want to hear more, so I left quietly.

One Fall evening, I went to Josie's apartment to ask if she wanted to take a walk. I wanted to tell her about a dream I'd had the night before. As we walked across the crisp leaves, I looked down and told her I had dreamed about her two children. They were safe and happy, standing together in a room I recognized as mine. She became serious and asked me to look at her while I told the dream. After I finished, she smiled and said she had dreamed about me too. She told the sisters at church that God showed her I was to be her husband. She admitted she had a crush on me since the first time she saw me and believed she would become my wife.

From that day forward, we both knew there was a connection. I hadn't dated anyone since high school, and she wasn't trying to date either—she stayed busy. We took a week to think about what we wanted to do. After two years of friendship, we decided to officially start dating. Six months later, we were married. It would've happened sooner if she hadn't wanted a June wedding. We were engaged within two months. It was her dream to marry in June, and her children loved me.

But something felt off. She didn't introduce me to her family until the day of the wedding—*during* the wedding. I wondered why she hid our relationship. It was a red flag.

# Chapter 11 – My Compatible Marriage to Josie

I was twenty-four when we married, and Josie was twenty-nine. While we were dating, she told me she'd been concerned about my age when we first met, and neither of us was sure if we were truly compatible. I told her my plan was to one day have two children of my own, but she already had two—each from a different man. One of those fathers was still active in his daughter's life with his lady friend. I never imagined starting a family like that, and she didn't picture building a life with a younger man until she got to know me, I was different.

After that conversation, we weren't sure we were right for each other. Even my brother Mitchell asked why I would marry a woman with two children who weren't mine. Josie and I walked away from one other that day not knowing if a marriage would ever happen. Her mother once told her that no good man would ever want her because she had two children, and Josie carried that wound for years—right up until the day I walked into church for the second time. Two days after our breakup, she called wanting to talk.

When we saw each other again, we hugged and kissed. She told me her children had been asking for me—especially little Lisa, who had fallen in love with me so strongly she fought other children who said they loved me too. Josie said she couldn't stop thinking about me, and that my age didn't matter anymore because she saw how loyal, godly, and mature I was. Her children loved me, and she admired how dedicated I was to my brothers at such a young age.

I felt relief hearing that from Josie. I told her I didn't mind her having two children if we could have one child together. She smiled and said yes. Then I asked about her relationship with Lisa's dad, the man I used to see at church. She told me nothing was going on between them and hadn't been for over a year. I held her hand and hugged her, and when she wrapped her arms around me she wouldn't let go, everything changed. We planned to wait until marriage to have sex but the time apart ended that promise.

We were married six months after we met on June 2, 1983. Three months later, we spent a week in Charleston, SC, for our honeymoon. We had a wonderful time. The ironic part was that the lady who originally invited me to church—the woman I thought I'd end up with—was the same one who drove us to Charleston and back because her family lived in the area which gave her the opportunity to visit.

Our sex life was passionate at first. During the honeymoon and after we came home, intimacy was frequent. But something began to bother me. I wasn't happy afterward, even though I made sure she was satisfied. Right after intimacy, Josie would shut down emotionally—getting up, putting on clothes, or wrapping herself tightly in the sheets so she wouldn't feel my touch. If I reached for her, she'd move away without a word. It made me feel like a stranger.

I didn't see that emotional problem coming. Nothing showed before marriage that she'd reject me afterward. Because of that, I imagined leaving within the first year. I refused to live a miserable life with a woman who couldn't love all of me—especially when I loved her so deeply. I asked her to tell me what was wrong because I felt rejected. She said nothing was wrong and that she loved me. I told her that wasn't true—you can't make love to me and then turn your back like nothing happened. We couldn't build a healthy marriage that way. I told her I wondered if she was bipolar, did I marry someone with a mental issue.

As we lay there talking, I felt her body trembling with fear. I told her I wouldn't be the same man she married if she refused to open up to me. I told her I didn't see this side of her until after we were married, and I wanted to know why she hid it—why she kept her family so secretive. I could feel myself becoming distant. That was part of my nature, and I wasn't going to change it for anyone.

Josie truly was a beautiful person, within and out. She was a loving mother, and my brothers adored her. She was thoughtful and kind—everything I needed in a wife except for those moments after intimacy and the times she tried to control me, which seemed ingrained in her. I told her I'd been rejected my whole life—especially by women—I refused to feel that same rejection from my wife during our sacred moments. It was spiritually damaging. I explained how her shutdowns were killing my desire for her.

She assumed I was so reserved that I wouldn't understand what she was doing—that she could control me emotionally. She didn't know the feelings building inside me because I rarely showed anger unless pushed. I was peaceful, so she mistook that for mental weakness. She wasn't satisfied with me being myself, and I wasn't satisfied with myself either— how did she expect me to handle living with a woman who felt the same way about me as I did?

I calmly told her not to push my emotions too far or she would see a side of me she wouldn't like. I would become distant and only relate to her when necessary—a defensive blueprint I'd built over a lifetime. I never imagined needing to use it in my marriage. Josie saw the change. I wasn't happy anymore, and I wasn't hiding it.

I had to learn to measure my life against the written word of God and lead my family the same way—something I learned from the late John Penny. Happiness was key to our survival. If we were happy together, we could overcome anything. We both knew I had a calling—not necessarily to preach, but to help people heal. I didn't fully understand that calling then because I still didn't like being myself. I wanted to be like John, and Josie noticed similarities. I studied the Bible during most of my free time that first year of marriage, and Josie lost patience with it. She grew frustrated when I took my Bible on trips because she wanted more attention, and I didn't understand that.

I told her God was first and head of our home. That's why we needed balance—she needed emotional balance, and I needed spiritual balance that we wouldn't harm one another. We didn't realize we were opening the door for psychological trauma to ruin our family life. I had to learn how to be myself with Christ consciousness—not religion.

The friction between us was spiritual and emotional, not personal. We both wanted the best for our lives but needed to face our past traumas. One night, during a passionate moment, I held her close so she wouldn't pull away. As we lay silently, the room felt peaceful. Suddenly she started speaking—softly, trembling, almost whispering beneath the sound of the music. It got my full attention. Her body shook as she talked. I held her with her head resting on my shoulder.

She told me she loved me for loving her children the way I did. I told her any sane person would love them—they were lovable. Then she told me something that broke my spirit. She said she hadn't introduced me to her mother because she felt her mother didn't love her—not even from birth. Josie had been left unnamed in the hospital nursery for a week or two until her aunt Mary came, named her, and took her home.

At sixteen, Josie was abducted by three men while walking to the bus stop in downtown Columbia, S.C. They held her in a house for a week, forcing her to cook, clean, and have sex. They all thought they broke her to become their slave after a week because she wasn't reported missing, therefore they went out to shop and left her alone which gave her a chance to escape. When she got home and told her family, they asked why she expected anyone to look for her. Her mother called her a prostitute. Josie said she was shattered by that but still respected her mother, though she distanced herself emotionally. Josie told me she thought her mother would say something to me I didn't like.

Her tears poured as she continued. She said the fathers of her children also forced themselves on her, and that's how she became pregnant both times. She never planned either pregnancy, but abortion never crossed her mind. She hated sex because of those experiences. She said she never enjoyed intimacy until she met me because she felt I truly cared about her. She loved that feeling more than she could explain.

She told me she'd never experienced the love she found in me, which is why she couldn't open up earlier—she feared I wouldn't marry her if I knew her past. I told her that wasn't true; my love for her and her children was deep and sincere. I wondered how I would help raise two children, but I always remembered the dream I'd had. She said she didn't want to do anything to damage our marriage anymore. She admitted her fault in trying to change me, thinking I wasn't vocal enough. She realized she couldn't change me without changing herself. She told me I needed to believe in myself, but her real struggle was fear—fear of losing a good man, something people told her she'd never have.

As she spoke, I recognized the chains of fear wrapped around her mind. We lay on one pillow as the scent of lavender oil filled the room. Then she told me her body was always weak because she was born with polio. She feared her mother would abandon her because of that. Her muscles hadn't developed properly. Running left her gasping, and climbing stairs was a struggle. She feared men would take advantage of her because of her slim frame—light-skinned, curvy, ninety-five pounds at five-foot-seven, with limited physical strength.

Her tears continued to flow. She said she'd had only one true best friend growing up. Some women were jealous of her shape. Her mental and physical weakness created an inferiority complex that kept her from loving herself until she accepted Jesus Christ as Savior two years before meeting me. Listening to her felt like looking into a mirror of my own life. I held her close and told her to relax—that everything would be okay. I needed to understand why she rejected me because I'd rejected myself for years. The only thing that gave me an edge over my own mind was my Christ-inspired consciousness—something Josie embraced because she saw my gift and felt the purity in my actions beyond my faults.

A peaceful presence filled the room—almost electric. I pushed the feeling aside and focused on Josie's pain. I told her I loved her but couldn't live with her rejecting me. She had to realize I wasn't the one who caused her trauma—I wasn't in her past life. I told her she had to embrace a new era. She cried harder, saying that made her feel even worse because all I'd given her was goodness, kindness, respect, hope, and love—and she was close to ruining it. I told her I felt the same except when I was disrespected because you can't love someone and disrespect them. I seriously believed she didn't understand that.

After I said that, I felt her change. She kept crying, but the trembling stopped. As she released those past traumas into the arms of someone who truly cared, I finally opened up about myself. I told her how I'd been rejected my entire life—seen as weak, dumb, ugly, unsuccessful. Rejected by girls and women who said I was too dark-skinned and too quiet. Mocked by jealous light-skinned guys. Rejected by my own father, who didn't include me in his will—I found out after he passed away. My siblings and I rented a car and drove to New Jersey to collect his belongings. His family already held a small viewing and cremation because we couldn't get there in time.

# Chapter 12 — I Wasn't Included in My Dad's Will

When we arrived at our dad's apartment in Jersey City, New Jersey, his brother—my Uncle Bishop Willy O. Pittman, a minister—was excited to see all of us together for the first time. Uncle Willy was sharp and handsome with a pleasant spirit, completely different from my dad. We talked for a while and he suddenly asked me to follow him into another room. He wanted to know what happened when my dad last visited me and my family.

I honestly couldn't recall anything unusual. Uncle Willy told me my dad claimed I had stolen money from him and disrespected him—which is why he wasn't leaving me anything. Everything was supposed to be divided among my other siblings. Hearing that hit me hard. The man told a lie. I told Uncle Willy the truth while trying to get over the shock. To this day, I still don't know how I got over that moment.

As I was talking, Josie sat up in the bed, stunned that my dad intentionally cut me out of his will. She said, "Your dad didn't leave you anything on purpose. That was mean and evil. You were the best son he had." Then she laid her head on my shoulder.

I explained that Dad didn't like carrying money, so he'd given me five hundred dollars to hold for him. I hid it in a spot only Josie knew about. I always kept our rent money there but forgot to tell her that the cash wasn't ours. When he came back a few days later, I went to get it and realized the money was gone. When I returned empty-handed, he asked where it was. I told him Josie deposited it because she didn't know it belonged to him. I called her immediately and told her to bring it home.

Dad was furious. He accused us of stealing from him. I explained again that Josie didn't know, because I forgot to tell her. I told him respectfully to come back in an hour and I'd have his money ready. We were both pissed because the whole thing blindsided me. He kept that grudge until the day he died.

Another incident bothered him too. He wanted to give money to our youngest daughter, Philnesha, but not her two siblings because they weren't biologically mine. I told him firmly that all three were my children, and if he gave something to one, he needed to give something to all. I wasn't going to let favoritism create jealousy in my home. He disagreed and left upset, but later returned with my brother Mitchell in the passenger seat—how ironic. Mitchell was the one who had cussed him out over the phone many times, calling him a no-good father who never gave us anything—not even a plate of beans. Our grandmother was the one who fed us.

Dad and Mitchell were alike in their harsh ways. I was nothing like them, and honestly, they deserved each other. When they pulled into the yard, Dad stayed in the car. Mitchell came inside to get the money. He asked to see Philnesha, so I called her out, and the other children followed. They got excited seeing how big and tall he was. He tried to hand money only to Philinesha. I asked if he planned to give to the others. He said no. Therefore I told him to keep it unless he intended to recognize all of them. They drove off, and I didn't hear from Dad again.

After I told Uncle Willy everything, he believed me instantly. He said Dad was always mean. When we rejoined the others, they were anxious to know what was going on. Uncle Willy told them what Dad wrote in the will and that I had been excluded. They were angry and wanted to know why. Uncle Willy calmed them down because it ruined the mood, saying he wouldn't honor the will because I was his child too, and leaving me out wasn't godly or right.

He said, "Y'all are his and Retha's children. He should've honored that."

My brothers felt bad and started looking for things I might want. I didn't want anything he owned. It wasn't to my taste. My youngest brother John found a bunch of records—albums, forty-fives, and a record player. They knew I loved music, so they got excited. I ended up taking the whole collection, even though most of it was blues and I wasn't a big fan.

I wondered if my dad didn't believe I was really his child. It didn't bother me as much as it could have, because I was determined to become the kind of father he never was. I was finding courage for my own life.

When I finished telling Josie everything, she stayed quiet until I told her that one of the men who claimed to be my father was actually a murderer. She sat straight up and in the bed shocked, saying, "A murderer? Your daddy?" Then she laid back laughing, and I laughed too. That day, we bonded deeply. She listened to me, and I listened to her cry. We realized we deserved each other's love and respect. Our laughter dried our tears, and the only thing left to do was have hot sex—which we did, and neither of us moved afterward.

My bed faced a second-floor window, and I could see the leaves on the trees outside. Suddenly I felt light, as if I were lying on a cloud lifting me above the treetops. I saw blue skies and clouds. I thought I was dreaming, but I finally told Josie. She said she felt the same thing. When I asked what she thought happened, she said, "We became one. Not because of a piece of paper—spiritually, today."

She was right. We had disagreements, but we never argued. We didn't let our children see anything like that. Our home had peace. But my job was another story—something I had to get over. Josie encouraged me to find work I actually liked. I told her I always wanted to be a fireman. She didn't want that because she feared it was too dangerous. I told her not to worry—firefighters are well trained—and I was going to apply because it was my dream job.

We disagreed so strongly that she called the pastor for guidance. Josie didn't want to live in fear, and I loved the idea of the job. The pastor told me that since I was married, I had to consider Josie's desires too. I reluctantly took his advice because I knew she wanted me safe. But that old blueprint of fear and self-doubt crept in. I could have stood my ground—I had worked there before and knew I could do it—but I didn't speak up for myself.

What I didn't tell them was that I applied for the job as soon as I turned eighteen and got called for an interview. But again, I let someone else's desires outweigh my own. At the time, it didn't feel selfish—it felt like keeping peace. So I went along with Josie and the pastor instead of believing in myself and following my dream. Her fear of losing me guided her judgment, and I understood that. I submitted to her concerns. It was one of the few times we didn't strike a balance in our twenty-nine years of marriage. Still, we cherished harmony, and our home stayed filled with peace and pure love.

# Chapter 13 — My Promotion Into Hell

I kept searching for peace at work, so I took a Phlebotomy class at Midlands Technical College—even though no one in the office believed I would pass. I earned my certification and became one of the most trusted phlebotomists for children and babies. After gaining experience, I was promoted to Coordinator. Some people thought I was too soft for the role because they mistook kindness for weakness, but I respected people and confronted issues privately when I needed to.

Twice on the weekend, I was the only person who clocked in, covering the entire Phlebotomy department because of call-outs. When a problem gets that serious, the on-call pathologist is contacted. Dr. William Armstrong was called in after a physician complained about the shortage. When he arrived, I was the only one there. My supervisor—the late A.J. Cox—was called in too. When they asked what was going on, I told them I was the problem—because I was the only one who came to work.

A year later, Dr. Armstrong asked me to come to his office. Immediately I thought, *What have I done now?* Instead, he told me they wanted to promote me to work doing autopsies because I had been the only one to show up on those critical days. He said they preferred to promote from within and offered me the opportunity. I told him I never dreamed of doing autopsies, but I was grateful. He explained I'd need anatomy and physiology, and photography before being hired. This opportunity came six years into my phlebotomy career.

Not long after, an ex office coworker pulled me aside and tried to convince me to report the bad experiences I'd had with them, saying they were now dealing with problems with an office leader. I asked why she expected me to help when she was one of the people who laughed at me during the very meeting where I tried to address that leader's behavior.

The next day, the lab director called me into his office and asked whether anything inappropriate happened to me in the main office. I was caught off guard because he specifically mentioned the morning I was rudely told not to come inside during their meeting. I asked how he knew. He said office staff had come to him with complaints about how they and I had been disrespected. He was furious and said that if it was true, he would fire the leader on the spot.

I told him it *was* true, but also reminded him that those same people laughed at me and offered no support. Now that they were fed up, they wanted to use my experience for their benefit. He said he was going to fire her. I asked him not to. I didn't want them feeling victorious on my behalf when they never stood with me.

I asked him to call her in, question her, and tell her I saved her job. I wanted her to remember God's love through me. He agreed. If they supported me at the right time, she would've been fired then. Today, she and I are friends who greet each other with love and respect. She was hired  a few years later into a new job that blessed her family. Proof that true love doesn't inflict harm; it fights for what's  right. Love has to fight for freedom in this world.

During this time, my brother Joe's health declined. He lived in an apartment near the church with Billy, but after two years he had to be admitted into a nursing home. The nerve disease they lived with was frightening. I feared it myself until I turned nineteen. Still, I supported all three of my brothers until each of them passed away after entering nursing homes. Joe passed away after six months. Billy was admitted four years later. John followed five years after that.

John married Caroline Pittman, and they had two sons: Johnathan and Donavan. Before their conditions became devastating, each of my brothers asked me to be the one person they wanted in the room before they became unresponsive. During this era, a major spiritual shift was happening. I was married, and Mitchell was my only remaining sibling. I saw him once a year during the holidays until the last year of his life.

He kept his distance, and I didn't hear from him during that final year. I knew something was wrong. After he passed, I learned from his physician that he had been diagnosed and treated for schizophrenia while in the Army before being honorably discharged. We didn't know that growing up, but it explained his behavior.

We thought he was just mean. If only we knew what he was fighting through his mind. Malree was correct about Mitchell before she passed, he wouldn't be able to achieve anything unless he changed his life. Mitchell was honorably discharged from the Army because of a letter he asked me to write on his behalf which was accepted by the military because of our brother's health.

Mitchell passed in 2006 from heart complications due to cardiomegaly an enlarged heart—something many people with schizophrenia succumb to. His death hurt me the most. While cleaning out his belongings, it hit me that I was the last one left alive in my family. I worked for hours alone, crying, trying to understand. I found nitroglycerin pills scattered across his bed—proof he knew he was having a heart attack but couldn't reach them in time. A neighbor saw him struggling to get to his car to drive to the ER across the street. He collapsed in the parking lot of his apartment building next to the driver's side door.

As an adult, I understood his blueprint better. He struggled to understand his own mind, the same way I struggled with my memory issues. We all had challenges, but I used to envy them anyway. My brothers showed me their love in different ways. Even Mitchell, unpredictable as he was, left small signs—like a new pair of tennis shoes still in the box inside his closet which was my size. He left me shoes.

Every family has issues, but the level of those issues determines how much peace and freedom get strangled until dysfunction starts to feel normal. People live out their blueprint. I used to despise the love people saw in me because cruelty was so familiar. I could feel the love and the hate people had for me. I learned to stay quiet until the right moment came to stand for dignity.

Mitchell lacked dignity, though not by choice. Two weeks after he passed, I received a letter from the South Carolina Department of Corrections asking me to bring ID to Human Resources. I never knew Mitchell worked there for years. The HR representative said she knew my family. She explained the woman Mitchell listed as his beneficiary wasn't next of kin and asked if I knew her name. I didn't, though I suspected why he chose her. I've always been righteous by nature; Mitchell chose dominance and negativity.

Every time he crossed that line, I confronted him. When I disagreed with his dark outlook, he spoke harshly and loud, trying to control the narrative. Two years before he died, during one of those disagreements, he told me success was coming to him and that when he died, he wouldn't leave me anything in his will. I didn't respond. I didn't care because he added nothing to my life. He added a non relative as his beneficiary which he knew was illegal for me to obtain nothing of his as he told me. He had the same mentality as our father.

My married life was wonderful. Josie encouraged me to be myself—she reminded me I didn't need to imitate anyone for God to use me. Doors opened for new job opportunities beyond my desire to be a fireman. Dr. Armstrong called me into his office and told me to meet with the new lab manager about the classes I needed at Midlands Technical College. I enrolled.

On the first night, the instructor said the anatomy and physiology course was for advanced students. We'd be tested on ten chapters a week, completing in one quarter what medical students at the University of South Carolina took two quarters to complete. Hearing that terrified me because of my memory issues. He warned that if anyone had been out of school for a while, they should transfer out and take the basic anatomy course next quarter.

After a week, I told him I was uncomfortable. I had been out of school for fifteen years and worked full-time. I explained my promotion depended on that course. He said I was in the wrong class and should take the basic anatomy course next quarter. There was still time to enroll. He told me to inform the lab director.

The next day, I explained everything to the director. She denied me the chance to switch. The job was paying for the course, and if I didn't pass, I wouldn't be promoted. Taking that class felt impossible, but I pushed myself—mainly because so many people wanted to see me fail. The hatred for me was confusing.

The material wasn't impossible, but the volume was overwhelming. I failed all but three lecture exams but excelled in the lab. My high lab grades balanced my lecture failures, giving me a passing C+. I was shocked. I took my transcript to the director. She looked at it and laughed at my "C+," then told me she would never hire me. She took my transcript, threw it into her desk drawer, slammed it shut, and ordered me out. I was traumatized and confused, they lied to me.

I passed a course I had no business being in—one taught to the Medical University of South Carolina medical students—because she forced me into it. Some people didn't want to see me succeed, they were filled with hate for me. They stereotyped me as dumb and incompetent. They didn't know me. I walked away feeling stripped of my dignity.

I told my wife, Josie. She stopped me mid-rant and told me not to let my job disturb our peace at home. She reminded me who I was: a godly man who could walk through fire without being burned. She told me to stand on faith, fight back with courage, and trust that God would place the right people in my path. That conversation changed everything.

Still, I struggled with loving myself. I questioned others' mindsets more than my own. I learned that religion doesn't make you love yourself—it only opens the door for you to begin. Around this time, I started having dreams I couldn't comprehend—similar to the ones I had as a child. That very night, I dreamed I stood in a deep pit on top of venomous snakes. They crawled beneath my feet, biting me. I felt the stings, but the poison had no effect. I didn't understand the dream then, so I nearly forgot about it.

As I grew, other people's negativity made me doubt myself again. I had to act.

The administration at that local organization opened an unbelievable opportunity for me. Autopsies became a dream. I knew I needed courage over fear. I told Dr. Armstrong about the conversation with the lab administrator. He said he would investigate and told me to be patient and not speak with anyone else.

I tried, but fear crept back in. I fought too hard for that promotion to tolerate disrespect. These were administrators and physicians treating me like this. I learned a hard lesson: education, wealth, and status don't dictate character. People are people—same origins, different choices.

Moving from department to department exposed the same spirits which are lower energies: hate, negativity, envy, jealousy, arrogance. I realized this was spiritual warfare. My fight wasn't against people but against something deeper. I had to apply spiritual principles, even though the situation traumatized my mind. These were supervisors, doctors, attorneys, pastors—titles didn't matter. People aren't devils, even if some act evil, their evil is by choice. Understanding that prepared me for anything people will do.

Still, being rejected from the autopsy position after passing the course felt like salt poured into an open wound. They told me not to go to the morgue anymore. That hurt deeply. When I gained the courage to ask why, the director said they wanted people with experience. There was nothing I could do. Josie was fed up about how I was being disrespected at work.

Praying didn't change the situation, but it strengthened me. I learned prayer isn't magic. It's powered by dignity, love, faith, humility, courage, freedom, and truth. I was angry, but it wasn't the time to show it. I felt disrespected on every level and couldn't share those thoughts with anyone but Emmanuel (God with us).

While working in the accessioning area, I received autopsy specimens from the pathologist assistants. I got to know everyone hired for the position I was promised. None of them were happy. All three resigned within a year. Then they hired a fourth person—someone who worked with me in phlebotomy. I overheard him telling a coworker he got the job because he had experience. I couldn't believe it. Everyone in pathology knew we had worked side by side, yet they gave him the opportunity instead of me. They used a lack of experience to keep me from being hired. I felt racially discriminated against. Every hire was Caucasian. Maybe it wasn't intentional, but emotionally, I believed it was.

I didn't tell anyone but my wife. She reminded me: what God has for you, no one can take. She encouraged me not to lose focus. I prayed, then started looking elsewhere. The strange thing was I didn't feel hostility toward anyone but myself. I didn't know what to do with my life because disrespect was hitting me from every direction. Later I thought if I went elsewhere I could experience similar situations or worse.

Disrespect is fueled by envy, jealousy, and hate. The only things strong enough to defeat those are courage, humility, love, and truth. I didn't ask Dr. Armstrong anything else. I didn't care anymore.

A week later, the guy they hired to do autopsies drew blood from the wrong patient and was fired immediately. He was supposed to start in pathology the following week.

Disrespect shows itself through envy and hatred. Pure love doesn't resemble disrespect. Kindness isn't weakness—it heals. I was learning to nurture my soul while living in hell. Hell is not just a place; it's a psychological state. And somehow, I walked through the fire without being burned—just like God said I would.

# Chapter 14 — The Shout That Changed Everything

I began looking for new job opportunities, and as I returned to the phlebotomy lab, I suddenly heard my name being shouted from the end of the hallway—about thirty yards away. It was the director of pathology. He told me to put my tray away and come to the morgue to help him with an autopsy. I didn't understand what was happening. He shouted again, telling me not to ask questions and that, from that day forward, I'd be doing autopsies. He said he would make sure my transition from phlebotomy to pathology happened without any problems. Which was an indication to me that people in high positions knew what was happening with me.

As he said all this, he stepped into the lab director's office—the door was open—and made sure she heard every word. She was the same person who once told me she'd never hire me.

After the autopsy, the lab director called me into his office. He explained the position and told me not to ask questions about what happened earlier. They had to fire the pathologist assistant the previous weekend and had no choice but to give me the opportunity. Not all the pathologists supported me, and I wasn't welcomed in the histology lab. The supervisor there labeled me incompetent because I didn't have the educational background.

Instead of being treated like the assistants before me, I was sent to the main lab to remove biohazard waste whenever I wasn't doing autopsies. When the training was finished, I worked every day for five years without a single day off—weekends and holidays included. Because of my dedication, the director of pathology added on-call pay to my salary. Over time, I gained favor with all the pathologists, including the forensic pathologist, Dr. Clay Nichols, who was hired about seven years after I was hired.

Clay was hired to lead the autopsy service, he's a Forensic Pathologist. He made me feel like we were equals in life and work. He was genuine. During a private lunch meeting, he asked me to call him Clay, not Dr. Nichols. I told him my history in the lab and about my spiritual journey—how I grew up, what I'd learned, and how I felt called to ministry through my family and church, even though I wasn't religious. He was amazed I stayed in that environment. He encouraged me, saying I was the first true Christian he had ever known, and he promised our relationship would always be meaningful and respectful.

Clay wasn't just a professional mentor; he was God-sent as Josie quoted years earlier, that God would place the right person in my life. After our lunch, he recognized that my spiritual understanding ran deep. I didn't have a high academic background, but I had wisdom and purpose. I didn't tell him about my memory issues—I was ashamed and didn't know how to explain it. I survived by relying on spiritual principles of love, truth, and peace that lived deep in my conscious and subconscious mind.

Once the pathologists got to know me, they were at peace with me. My personality, work ethic, and passion for life spoke for themselves. I eventually became the lead autopsy assistant and trained others. Clay, along with Dr. Armstrong, Dr. Edward Catalano, and Dr. Larry Kline, became trusted friends. I wasn't on their level intellectually or financially, but I valued them—and I learned to value myself. Even though they lived privileged lives, they weren't arrogant. They understood my experiences as a Black man because of our private conversations.
*(This is where Step 4 of my Shadow Program applies: Value.)*

It felt incredible to be accepted for who I am. They could recognize my spiritual calling to help people heal. Dr. Catalano often said everything is relative. And though they were geniuses, they still desired spiritual growth—the same growth they recognized in me. We realized we were alike from within. The only difference was that their intellectual gifts made them wealthy.

I was born with the gift to help people heal, even though I didn't yet know how to heal myself—or how to overcome my memory issue. That "issue" wasn't the real problem; the real problem was me not accepting my inner self. I started holding counseling sessions during my work breaks, which became a blessing. People saw the spiritual gift within me. We met for prayer daily in the chapel, and I finally understood that my calling wasn't to preach or pastor but to help people—and even animals—heal.

Clay made life easier. He understood my frustration with not being accepted because of my educational background and quiet personality. He told me that having a college degree doesn't make you smart—how you apply knowledge does. He said when educated or intellectual people use their intelligence to belittle others, they expose their own ignorance. I told him I was tired of the discrimination I'd faced since day one—mostly because I was quiet and reserved. But my actions and work ethic always showed who I really was: a normal, respectful person.

People later confided in me that some staff assumed I was incompetent because I didn't have a degree. Before Clay was hired, the pathology group planned to hire a certified pathologist assistant. Someone who could help gross in histology because work was increasing and the histology technician didn't want me in histology, she would come to me after each meeting to "inform" me that my job was in jeopardy and that a new assistant would replace me from autopsies. She said this more than once, always with the intention to intimidate me with a lie.

The second time she tried it, I finally spoke up. I told her I'd had enough of the disrespect and harassment, and that if she ever bothered me again, I would take it to the organization's highest office—someone who knew me personally. She smirked and said going over the director's head would get me fired.

I told her plainly, "Why would I go to him when you twist situations before the truth can be heard? You will leave this job before I will. I'm done tolerating your behavior." She walked away. She resigned a year later.

I informed the supervising pathologist that the department was heading toward chaos if they didn't address the problems the histology technician was causing. He didn't believe me. Her intelligence and professional knowledge blinded him to her cruelty.

Several coworkers later came to me privately, in tears, saying they met with the pathologist and with her—they left feeling worse than before they went into the meeting. They apologized for not listening when I advised them not to meet with her. She was cunning and manipulative. They told me they planned to resign and not return the next day for the sake of their mental health and family life.

The next morning, I walked into an empty department. The director came in, noticed the work unfinished, and demanded to know what was going on. I told him I was the only one that showed up. He stormed off, yelling for the supervising pathologist. When that pathologist arrived, he asked me what was happening, and I reminded him of our conversation a month earlier. Dajavu! Once again but in a different department I'm the only employee that came to work although I was being cast out.

All those employees came to me earlier in tears, questioning their worth because they couldn't believe they could be treated so cruelly and it be allowed. These were highly educated people being treated like children. They asked how I endured such degrading treatment. They were Caucasian coworkers who knew they were capable and valuable, but the environment was crushing them. They felt the spirit in me—my peace, my songs, my positive words, my truth, my love—and that's why they came to me. I helped them heal psychologically.

I told them it takes courage to believe the truth, just as it takes courage to believe and live a lie. A lie embeds itself in the will and becomes emotional. That emotion can't satisfy the truth of who you are, which is why people stay lost within themselves. Freedom is tied to truth. They all thanked me for inspiring them and helping them heal, however they couldn't remain at that job because it hurt them deeply. I told them the most High was with me, I praised him for keeping me through his powerful love by faith.

Clay took my voice further than I could. In a group meeting, he explained everything I endured and made it clear things needed to change. It took courage to speak out, especially when I felt alone. I didn't know about the EEOC back then. All I had was my faith. I was already living the Shadow Program, even though I didn't have a name for it yet. It's effective now because it saved me then—through the wisdom of Yeshua, which helped me wake up the souls of people willing to hear the truth. I spoke truth to power.

My battle wasn't against people but against the powers and principalities of this dark world and spiritual wickedness in high places. My weapons weren't physical but spiritual—pulling down strongholds of the mind, starting with my own fear.

It wasn't easy. I fought hard to protect my peace. My faith grew because of the love I received from people in the lab. Word spread about the spiritual power and wisdom that helped others through me. I was learning my purpose before I fully realized it. Freedom begins with self-awareness and with understanding the purpose woven into the core of your DNA.

# Chapter 15 — The Miracle Chapter

The church we were part of began growing so quickly that we started looking for a new building—until the pastor turned away from teaching the truth and started using Scripture to serve his own twisted desires. The revival that week was powerful. The services were electrifying, and people returned every night hungry for more. But by the end of the week, those services were running far too late for families and for people who had to work early the next morning. We stayed because lives were being moved by the Holy Spirit, but something felt off.

After those late-night services, the pastor and one of the deacons—both married—began visiting members' homes at unreasonable hours. One night, they knocked on our door. My wife and I refused to open it. We spoke through the door because the visit felt suspicious. The pastor announced he was there to inform us that the man with him had been ordained as a deacon that evening. Josie told them that although the man had good intentions, he was still a babe in Christ and shouldn't have been ordained without approval from all the leaders.

I told them it was too late for a visit, and something in my spirit didn't feel right.

The next evening, we arrived early at the pastor's home for the leadership meeting. He wasn't there, but his wife—one of Josie's closest friends—was. She urged us to leave before he returned. The urgency in her voice stopped me in my tracks. I asked what was going on, she seemed frightened and saddened. She told us to sit down but be ready to leave—and to warn others.

Fear filled the room. My spirit already sensed something was wrong. The services had become emotional rather than spiritual as well.

Then she revealed the truth.

She said the pastor hadn't slept in a week. He'd been running around during the day, visiting graveyards at night, having an affair with a church member, and depositing and withdrawing money daily. We were stunned. She said he planned to seduce certain single women in the church. Then she handed us a sheet of paper—an abortion agreement between the pastor and a church member.

Josie and I read it together. Tears streamed down the pastor's wife's face. She said she loved us too much to hide the truth because she knew our love for Yeshua was genuine.

I feared for her safety. Our bond with her broke, but our respect remained. She put God first, even though the man in question was her husband. Earlier in ministry, that same pastor taught us that love and respect go hand in hand. He taught that if someone claims to love you while knowingly disrespecting you, that "love" is emotional and conditional.

He was preaching his own downfall.

That same night, Josie and I called John and Melissa Penny and told them not to go to the pastor's house. We met at their home instead and shared everything. John suggested a secret meeting with a few members to decide what to do. We chose to warn as many people as possible—and leave the church.

A few weeks later, half of us visited a mixed-race congregation on Forest Drive in Forest Acres, Columbia, S.C. People called it "the underground church" because the sanctuary sat below street level. The entire church welcomed us with open arms. John knew some of the members, and we all wanted something different—something pure.

During the prayer meeting, we testified about how God's love carried us through spiritual warfare. Our souls already belonged to God, therefore we defeated the satanic system of the previous church—even though we walked away with spiritual wounds and scars from leaving something we helped build.

The leadership at Forest Drive Baptist Church prayed for our healing. They recognized we were well-versed in Scripture, proven by our faith. The late John Penny was a living testimony of that and helped shape my character. Within a year, we were known as prayer warriors because we knew how to use the Word of Yeshua while praying for people. We were chosen for prayer teams, led home Bible studies, and served in care ministries. I played drums on the praise and worship team, and my son Cornelius played trumpet.

We were members of Forest Drive Baptist Church for thirteen years. It wasn't a traditional Baptist church—the pastor and leaders sought a deeper spiritual experience led by the Holy Spirit. There were frequent revivals and unity services with other churches. My family and I grew spiritually in ways we never expected. But inside, I still battled self-rejection. I doubted my intelligence and struggled with unbelief in myself, even though I was maturing spiritually.

Meanwhile, the autopsy room became a place where people came to me for private counseling—an office within an office. I wasn't a pastor; I was helping people survive the fears of life. Relationships, marriages, family issues, church hurt—nothing was off-limits. I learned from my own mistakes and by observing the patterns in people's lives. Everything begins in the mind—being present, avoiding confusion.

Certain experiences helped me overcome the failures tied to my memory struggles. I always felt chosen by Emmanuel (God with us), even as a child, though I didn't understand it. The opportunity to learn autopsies was a miracle itself. And through that, I met an elderly cleaning woman who wasn't afraid to clean the autopsy area. She was about sixty-two but worked with the strength and speed of someone decades younger.

One day she came in while I was finishing a case and asked if she could rest. She looked exhausted. I told her yes. When I turned back around, she had fallen asleep. I let her rest. When I woke her gently, she said she was worried she wouldn't be able to retire. She told me she trusted me like a son—a true Christian. Then she confessed she couldn't read or write.

People looked down on her, but she wasn't ashamed. God had blessed her with a steady job and the ability to pay off her home. She relied on the bus to get everywhere. Then she shared her past—how her father, who wasn't her biological parent, abused her daily as a child. All she ever wanted was acceptance and love.

She told me her whole story—years of abuse, hardship, and survival. And she praised God that someone finally listened without judgment. She said she sometimes felt weak and sinking inside and feared she wouldn't retire because she "couldn't get her money." Her supervisors tried to help but got nowhere. She lost hope for years. I felt deep compassion and told her I would help.

Over the next few days, we made calls to Vital Records and the Social Security Administration. They said I had to be next of kin to obtain certain information, so we had to go in person. Our supervisors let us leave early after my cases were done. When we met with the SSA representatives, my friend told them she trusted only me. She had a learning disability that affected her reading and writing. The representatives didn't know this—she looked "normal," but I was her anchor.

Helping her became a turning point in my life.

She taught me to value myself because she valued herself despite everything she had to endure.

The autopsy room became a place of healing for doctors, nurses, and security staff from all backgrounds. I learned to combine spiritual wisdom with positive reinforcement. I helped people understand fear, death, and how to live a balanced life spiritually and practically. I prayed and meditated for guidance to help my elderly friend because each day grew more challenging.

Eventually, we discovered the real problem: she had two different birthdates in the retirement and Social Security systems. She was sixty-six. She started working at Columbia Hospital at seventeen, back in 1965. Her medical records confirmed her age through her daughter's birthdate and her employment history.

But when the representative questioned why she couldn't remember her birthdate, my friend misunderstood it as mockery. Her temperament shifted to anger, once that happened she was hard to deal with. The meeting began slipping away.

I asked myself what to do. I focused deeply. If we walked out she wouldn't be able to retire.

Then the answer came as I meditated.

I asked the representative to step into the hallway. I explained quietly that my friend had a learning disability that affected her understanding and her ability to read and write. The representative's eyes softened. Suddenly, everything made sense to her. It was found that my friend endured a lot of abuse which made her temperamental at moments.

She hugged me and thanked me for helping someone so faithfully. I told her, "God is good."

When we returned, she stepped away briefly. When she came back, she was smiling—my friend's retirement was approved. All we needed was a corrected birthdate from the Department of Transportation. It was one of the happiest days of our lives. Her entire department celebrated. Her supervisors were shocked—they thought the situation was hopeless.

I drove her home that day, but she wasn't in good spirits. She told me she was angry because she thought she overheard me telling the representative she was "retarded." My heart sank. I explained that I never said that. I told the representative only that she had a learning disability—nothing more. That truth had set her free. But she was still hurting—pride and pain ran deep within her subconscious mind.

I haven't seen her since her retirement celebration ten years ago. My season in her life ended. Sometimes God places us in someone's life for a moment to fulfill a divine purpose. That season was a miracle. I was led by the Holy

Spirit, and I could feel the presence of Yeshua guiding us.

During that same era, my wife developed what we thought was a lung illness—something that would eventually require me to retire early, even though I didn't have the age or time. Josie had been quietly struggling with breathing issues for a year, even as I was helping my elderly friend. She hid her fear from me and wouldn't let me accompany her to appointments until I noticed how out of breath she became after our intimate moments.

I was also stressed. Something felt wrong in my own body. No matter how much I warmed up or stretched before workouts, I strained my right shoulder, neck, and hip—just like in high school. I knew I needed healing. So I approached a friend who worked in engineering and taught karate. I told him what I was feeling physically and mentally.

I thought karate might help strengthen me. Spiritually, I was strong, but I was absorbing stress from circumstances beyond my control. Even though the stress was emotional, I became more conscious of my will and the consequences of reacting out of emotion.

I was built for this life—but at the time, I didn't realize the fire of life's situations wouldn't consume me.

# Chapter 16 — Josie's Passing

Josie and I were married for thirty-three years. We had three children—Cornelius, Willisha, and Philnesha. Cornelius was eight, Lisa was two, and Philnesha was born the following year after we got married. Ours was a solid marriage until death. I didn't understand the depth of her love for me until she was gone.

About a month after her service, I visited a store in Columbia, S.C. called Solomon's Temple. I used to shop there often with a few close friends. Two women I knew approached me that day, excited. They told me they had known my wife, but never realized I was the man she always spoke so highly of. They said it only clicked after hearing me preside over her service.

Josie's energy was powerful. She made sure I would be the one to speak over her body. She passed in February—the month she was born. Her service was delayed a day because of snow, and even though the storm stopped, the roads were still icy. The minister who was supposed to preside got snowed in and didn't call me, which I considered disrespectful. I wasn't feeling well myself—Josie passed her cold to me, the same cold she caught from Tyler, our youngest grandson.

When it came time for the speaker and the minister still hadn't shown, the funeral director tapped my shoulder and whispered, "You do it. I've heard you speak here before. You can do it."

I was completely caught off guard, but I knew it was exactly what Josie would have wanted. I was the only one who truly knew the "new Josie." She talked to me about the spiritual things we were experiencing together, especially the music that soothed her when gospel songs no longer could. She chose the music for her service because she used it for her daily healing. She hoped at least one person would be blessed by it.

The woman at Solomon's Temple told me how deeply Josie loved me. She described me as a handsome, strong, spiritual man who cared for his wife and children. They said she taught them how to love, how to be loved, and how to be strong, godly women and mothers. She lived the character of the virtuous woman in Proverbs 31. Once they realized I was her husband, everything made sense—they saw me come into the store alone for years and never connected us. People were genuinely excited to learn Josie was my wife.

Around our twenty-fifth year of marriage, Josie began experiencing frequent shortness of breath. She was born with polio, which left her muscles underdeveloped. She wasn't physically strong—light-skinned, spiritually sharp, naturally curvy, but never more than ninety-eight pounds at five-foot-seven until the illness caused her to gain weight.

We spent thirteen years as members of Forest Drive Baptist Church. Together with Brennon Guy, a member of another church, the late Henry Stokes Jr., Minister Burnard Green, the late Thomas Hickman, and Michael Belz, we had a boarding home ministry called South Carolina Outreach Ministry. We held Bible study, praise and prayer sessions, and collected offerings among ourselves to help the elderly we served.

One elderly woman lived alone with no electricity and damaged floors. Her son lived nearby but didn't care for her. We paid her bills and hired someone to repair her floors. She passed a year later, however before she passed she told us God sent us because she was sick and nobody knew. For about two years, we dedicated one evening each week to help people across Columbia and the surrounding counties. Pure Love, Value, and Courage were our guiding principles—principles that healed us as much as the people we served. Healing always swings both ways.

Josie handled most of our family affairs as a stay-at-home mother until our oldest reached high school. Then she decided she wanted to work again. She earned her cosmetology license from Kenneth Shuler Beauty School and rented a booth at Columbia Beauty Salon under Mrs. Eloise Gaines. She loved doing hair and became close friends with Mrs. Gaines. After years of working, she began having trouble inhaling certain chemicals—issues she'd never had before. We talked and eventually decided she should retire for health reasons.

During those years, we experienced powerful spiritual growth at Forest Drive Baptist. I danced, played drums, and served on the worship team. Josie and I were on the prayer team, and worship was our lifestyle at home. We heard speakers like Dr. Tony Evans, the late Dr. Myles Munroe, the late Christian artist Carman, and the late Prophet Leland Davis. We were so involved in ministry that we didn't realize how serious her breathing issues were becoming.

Forest Drive Baptist was known for tent revivals that brought local churches together. I served as a deacon and on the worship team during those events. Minister Leland Davis was a humble servant—never calling himself a prophet, though he carried a powerful anointing. After one tent service that deeply moved the congregation, Pastor Glen Anderson asked me to escort Minister Davis to the church office. I had the keys that night.

Inside, I told him he had been a blessing to the people. He replied, "I'm a servant. All I want is to do the Father's will." He was in his seventies, gifted in understanding the Book of Revelation, and had traveled the world ministering. He asked my name. When I told him "Phillip," he asked if I was married. The moment I said Josie's name, he remembered the prophetic word he had spoken over us earlier.

Then he asked me to sit with him for a few minutes. The room grew quiet and heavy as I listened. He told me about his wife—their ministry, their travels, and how deeply he loved her. Then he shared what he discovered months earlier: he came home to find his bank account emptied and all his belongings gone. She deceived him from the beginning. He said she had been sent to destroy him, like Jezebel in the Bible. He wept as he spoke, and I trembled, unsure why he was telling me such personal things.

He told me the FBI and CIA had watched and questioned him for years, attending his services openly and in secret. His anointing drew attention.

Years before his death, the manner of his passing had been revealed to him in a dream—a fatal car accident. He didn't know it was about him at the time, but later understood. A few years after that dream, he was killed in a head-on collision caused by a drunk driver.

Before he died, Pastor Anderson arranged a private meeting between us because of a dream I had—one in which Minister Davis was coming to Columbia. Pastor Anderson hadn't spoken to him in years and didn't believe me at first. But six months later, he called Josie and me into his office to confirm that Minister Davis was returning for a revival as an unlisted speaker. That dream came to pass. Pastor Anderson told me God had clearly chosen me and that my prophetic dream shocked him.

About a year after meeting Minister Davis, I began sensing a call out of the church system. I saw hypocrisy in some of the predominantly white churches we visited. I questioned Christianity because of the racial politics I witnessed among pastors. I saw qualified Black men and women passed over for leadership roles in mixed congregations. Minister Davis, though Caucasian in appearance and from another country, told me he didn't see race when ministering. He said God sees His original people and His image in them. Race has no place in God's house.

I asked him to speak to my pastor about the issue. He said, "I came here for you. I can't tell a man how to run his own house unless the Holy Spirit directs it." His wisdom stayed with me. I learned to seek wisdom, pursue it, and apply it—even when it made me appear weak. That became part of what I call my Shadow Program.

He also told me, "If your peace isn't received, keep it to yourself. Shake the dust off your feet and move on which means clear your mind. Let your life speak the truth." Two years later, I knew I was being called to leave the church system. I followed that path because of the spiritual jealousy I experienced from some church members. The church system was filled with jealous people.

It didn't matter the race or sex. I warned them their jealousy would destroy them because I refused to be jealous of another person's gift. This was the era  I applied courage and truth which became part of my Shadow Program. I felt alone, but I obeyed consciously where we needed to be.

Two years later, Josie's sister Joy and her husband, Pastor Robert Vanlue, invited us to join their new church. They offered me the role of assistant pastor and drummer. After a year of serving, the congregation grew, and I was ordained into the prophetic ministry for our congregation because of my genuine love for God's people. The ministry required discipline, sacrifice, prayer, and study. By then, I had been in ministry for sixteen years.

We served with the Vanlues for three years before I was led to start my own ministry—an in-home gathering free from the traditional church system of control. During that time, Josie flourished in her calling to help women find freedom within themselves and their relationships.

My calling wasn't to pastor a church—it was to heal consciousness and awaken God's people. We loved being in a place where people could grow spiritually. Our church began around the time of the 9/11 attacks, and people were searching for answers. We studied America's true biblical identity—knowledge I couldn't share in other churches. We named our fellowship Fresh Wind Tabernacle.

A friend, Satep El Bey (Timothy Johnson), introduced me to the Moorish Science Temple of America, founded by Noble Drew Ali. I attended several meetings and learned about the Moors, whose history had been erased from

American education. Noble Drew Ali followed the teachings of Yeshua and wrote the Holy Koran Circle Seven, revealing Christ's true life and identity which connected us not to curse us as a people. That knowledge shook everything I knew about Christianity and explained the calling I felt to come out of that system.

The classes were full of people angry to learn they were still considered slaves under the law—a truth Drew Ali exposed. He revealed that our identity had been erased by colonial rule and systemic racism. I learned that George Washington wasn't the first U.S. president—John Hanson, a Moor (African), was. In fact, the first six presidents of the new nation were of Moorish descent. Why was this hidden from me until I turned fifty years of age? I learned that my ancestors weren't slaves. People were angry to find we were lied to from birth unless our family were educated about our identity as Native Americans before the Europeans came in ships.

During that time, I discovered my Cherokee bloodline—something it took fifty years to uncover. My Aunt Edith Richardson confirmed it before passing at 103 years old.

I researched everything and shared it with my family. Learning the truth changed how I understood our spiritual existence. Our ancestors weren't born slaves—they were divine people from a divine order. Some members of Forest Drive Baptist told me my race was cursed, but I told them I wasn't cursed—I was chosen and highly favored. I asked them how true Christians could look me in the eye and say something like that because of the color of my skin which is the indication we all were being spiritually misguided with a passion for lies.

I told them my first purpose was to remember who I am—an identity stolen in 1776 by the CORPORATION known as the UNITED STATES OF AMERICA, a system that created lies to strip African people of their identity and justify slavery under international contract law. How could such a system be Christ-like? It didn't match the truth.

Something deep within me was searching for a truth I didn't know existed until Satep El Bey (Timothy Johnson) told me about the Moors in 2009. That conversation reconnected me to my spiritual roots. It awakened my soul beyond religion. I realized life existed far beyond what I could see. That lie was created to keep me blind to my true self.

After learning the truth about my original identity, I legally changed my name to reflect my original African heritage. Osaze carries a dual meaning—"loved by God" in African and "loved by the Lord" in Hebrew. Bey means "law giver of the land." If that was my lineage, why was my identity erased from my mind?

I felt both fear and excitement—two sides of the same energy, depending on where the mind focuses. I was afraid of losing Christian friends and family because I didn't yet know enough about the true history of my people. Biblically it is written: "My people are destroyed for lack of knowledge because they reject knowledge." If we reject spiritual truth, how can Yeshua receive us?

I was being drawn into Moorish enlightenment—exactly the calling I had been searching for. I kept knocking on different doors as I grew in understanding, building everything on the foundation of Biblical truth. Rejecting knowledge of self only leads to self-destruction.

The doors that opened for me included teachers of yoga, Tai Chi, meditation, and prayer. I was led by the Spirit of Truth to a bookstore I had driven past for years without ever stopping. One Saturday afternoon, I passed it again on my way home, glanced at the building, and suddenly felt a burning in my abdomen leading me to turn around and go inside the store.

The moment I stepped through the door, I was greeted by a kind, respectful African woman in her mid-to-late sixties. “Welcome to Seven Rays Bookstore. May I help you?” Her name was Sis. Victoria Hampton. We began talking instantly—like we knew each other in another lifetime. We both felt it. I told her what made me turn the car around, and from that moment forward, we became close friends until her passing.

She later told me she was drawn to my spirit because I didn’t talk or act like other Moors she met; my mind was open and becoming balanced. She recognized what my soul was searching for and invited me back the next evening for the weekly class she taught.

Sis. Victoria’s store was beautiful and powerful. She didn’t just sell spiritual and inspirational books—she carried healing oils, candles, music CDs, and everything that builds consciousness from within. She taught from the “I AM” Activity of the Saint Germain Foundation, giving her students “I AM” decree booklets and discourses. The more I learned from her, the more we realized we were predestined to meet at that exact point in our lives. She loved my desire to help people heal and admired the devotion I had for my ailing wife. I admired her passion for helping others, especially young women rebuilding their lives. She purchased and renovated a house to shelter them. She was a wonderful person and teacher, so I brought people from our ministry to her store. They all loved her.

People in our ministry also loved the direction we were moving—beyond traditional church order. I encouraged everyone to grow spiritually without judging what wasn't "mainstream religion" or what they didn't understand. Our meditation sessions were refreshing. People walked in stressed and walked out renewed. One woman's transformation was so noticeable that her husband grew jealous. He thought she was having an affair with me because she returned home peaceful and happy. To him, the only thing that could make a woman change like that was sex.

He asked to meet me. We arranged a lunch meeting at work, since his wife and a female co-worker—whom I'll call Co-worker One—attended our gatherings regularly. When he and I met, he said he felt something different about me. I invited him to our next meeting and told him about the bookstore that had been such a blessing. We became friends, and he later began inviting his own friends.

But jealousy soon entered the picture.

A second co-worker—Co-worker Two—created a lie about me and Co-worker One. Josie warned me something like this could happen. Co-worker Two, who was best friends with Co-worker One, became jealous because she and I were once attracted to each other as teenagers—though nothing ever came of it.

Co-worker One didn't know her friend was feeding lies to her husband, and the two of them talked daily. I learned about the situation when her husband called, saying he needed to speak with me. I was caring for my wife, but I agreed to talk briefly.

He began by calling me a humble man. Something in his tone put me on edge. Then, without warning, he accused me of being a fraud and a liar. Before I could respond, he accused me of sleeping with his wife. I was too shocked to react quickly.

He continued, saying a "reliable source" told him I was taking his wife on dates and having sex with her because she was "fine" and my wife was "fat, ugly, and out of shape." He said he thought I was a true man of God. "What do you have to say now, preacher?"

I told him I didn't care what he thought of me. I hadn't touched his wife or any other woman. And I told him plainly: I loved the "fat, ugly, out-of-shape" woman I was with. He insisted I was taking his wife to motels. I said, "Prove it." His excitement made it clear he wanted to damage my reputation. I told him I didn't know where he got such nonsense and that he had disrespected my wife—someone dealing with illness. When I reminded him of that, his energy changed.

I asked him why would I be stupid enough to take his wife to motels in broad daylight while I was scheduling sessions with Sis. Victoria and helping people in our ministry grow beyond traditional Christianity. He asked again if I was sure I had no idea what he was talking about. I said, "Hell no. And don't call me or come near me again." Then I hung up.

I told Josie what happened. She wasn't surprised. She reminded me she warned me what some women would do when they wanted a man. I was naïve about women's attraction to me, and she knew it. She asked how I felt. I told her that if the man had been standing in front of me, he would have met a part of me nobody knew from my younger fighting days—and we both would've been hurt. The only thing that stopped me was knowing I could end up in jail or dead, unable to care for her.

After that call, I continued communicating with the two women at work, but the relationship changed. I stayed at peace, but I was disappointed that Co-worker One said nothing to me about her husband's accusations.

The next week, the husband called again—this time to apologize. He said I was the most humble and righteous man he'd ever met. I told him the damage was already done because his words struck the consciousness of an innocent, ill woman he never once considered. If his misunderstanding had been aimed solely at me, I could have let it go. But he believed a lie and harmed others because of it.

Minister Davis taught me to use jealousy—not let jealousy use me. He said jealousy is a defensive emotion meant to protect, not destroy. He told me never to be jealous of another man's gift unless that gift harms your life. "Let your jealousy be righteous," he said.

From him, I learned to watch out for jealous men. Ego can make them jealous of anything—attention, women, money, another person's abilities. And when jealousy is directed at someone's gift, the anger isn't really toward the person... it's toward God, the one who created the gift.

The husband admitted he suspected his wife of cheating long before she met me, and that Co-worker Two told him I was sleeping with her. He said jealousy drove both of them. I accepted his apology, but I told him he shouldn't have disrespected my wife's health condition. That crossed a line. My consciousness was on fire because she deserved honor.

The following week, I finally approached Co-worker One and asked if her husband spoke to her about our phone call. She said no and wanted to know why I was asking. When I told her everything—how Co-worker Two had started the entire situation—she became visibly upset. She left her desk, called her husband, and then confronted Co-worker Two. The argument that followed ended their friendship permanently.

I introduced everyone to Sis. Victoria's store and the "I AM" teachings because they already carried that inner violet fire—they just weren't conscious of it yet. The awakening had to come from within. Our class loved her guidance because it connected back to the same spiritual foundation they already knew from Christianity: the spirit within. They were learning not to judge or elevate Christianity above other religions and cultures. They were learning they were the head and not the tail by shifting their consciousness from negativity to positive living. We were learning to apply faith—not just speak it.

One visitor from our ministry grew jealous because her schedule didn't allow her to join us at Sis. Victoria's store or the African shop. Out of that jealousy, she called another woman's husband and told him his wife was having an affair with me, conscious of the damage she entented to cause.

During this time, I was discovering the importance of value—valuing myself, my gift, and the mission in my life. Sis. Victoria planted that mindset in me. Josie used to teach the women how to value themselves in their marriages and relationships, how not to lose themselves by focusing so heavily on their men but to nurture themselves as well.

Around then, I developed constant neck, shoulder, and back pain and couldn't understand why. I approached a coworker, Sensei Rod Gardner, who worked in engineering and was a black belt in karate. I told him what I was dealing with and that I thought learning karate might help heal my mind, body, and spirit. We talked for a few minutes to get to know each other. He told me he had observed me for years and saw the respect people had for me. Because of that, he invited me to his dojo—DoJo Nishi in Lexington, S.C.

I trained there for seven years and earned my first-degree black belt in Suri-Ryu Karatedo, an Okinawan style. Classes were led by Sensei Gardner, Sensei Chestnut, and Dr. Jimmy A. Duensing, Shodan. After six years I earned my brown belt. The discipline helped me deeply. But during that same time, Josie's health worsened.

In addition to Josie's breathing issues, she began experiencing severe back pain. She usually didn't want me to take off work to accompany her to appointments, but one day she asked me to go. Her physician told us she had COPD—a terminal lung disease. He explained that her back pain came from scoliosis which developed at birth and that her lung condition started early because of polio. Even though she lived normally for years, complications were almost certain later in life. The news was devastating to me—but at least we finally had answers.

Josie already knew, but she kept it from me to protect me because she didn't know how I would react. She hid it for an entire year. The only question going through my mind once I found out was how was I going to take care of her.

Her pain grew so severe she couldn't drive anymore. This was hard for her because she had always been active. Her health became my top priority. Sensei Gardner and a few dojo brothers helped me build a ramp to the bedroom door for Josie's walker and wheelchair. I placed a refrigerator and everything she needed into her room. She had to use an oxygen tank daily, which doubled our electric bill. The stress felt like fire inside of my body every night when I tried to sleep.

I needed more income, therefore I studied to become an insurance agent. When I took the first exam, something felt wrong. After answering ten questions, I told the instructor, "I think I'm taking the wrong test." She checked and discovered the lead agent had given me the wrong exam information. Since I already answered ten questions, I had to finish—even though I hadn't studied for it. I guessed every answer. It took two more attempts to finally pass the proper exam.

That struggle reminded me of my third- and fourth-grade years when I failed at everything. Old memories rushed back through my mind, and I didn't know how I was going to hold myself together emotionally.

One day, while caring for Josie, she asked why her friends weren't coming to see her. I was always able to answer her questions, but not this one. She didn't know what I was dealing with—her illness, my stress, the declining vision in my right eye. I told her to rest while I went to the restroom,  instead I went to the bedroom and cried. Her question broke something within me because I knew the truth.

All I could honestly say was that she had me.

As I stood there wondering what to do, the weight of everything pressed on my shoulders and legs. But I refused to break. As I meditated, I felt energy flow through my body. The heaviness left, but the thoughts remained. I pushed the negative thoughts aside and remembered how many times we had been there for our friends. Reality set in: people are different. Our friends weren't built like we were. In two years, the only visitor Josie received was Mrs. Eloise Gaines, owner of Columbia Beauty Salon. That truth gave me a strange kind of peace.

When I returned, Josie asked, "Darling, what took you so long?" I told her I understood why her friends weren't coming—they didn't know how to handle seeing you like this. She said, "I'm still me." I asked if she wanted me to call them. She said, "No. I want them to come on their own."

God sent her comfort through our son Cornelius's girlfriend, Nyaree Patterson. We didn't know her before she started dating Cornelius, but she became a true blessing. She helped with everything—no strings attached. Josie valued and loved her deeply.

Josie was still herself consciously, however she refused to become bitter. She wanted to see her friends again before she passed. I told her people were dealing with their own emotions, and no matter what, we would get through everything together.

Her doctor prescribed steroids, which made her gain weight and retain fluid in her legs and feet—early signs of congestive heart failure. She gained over fifty pounds. Her body wasn't built to carry that. We told the physician the medication was harming her and we will no longer use it. Once we stopped, she felt better.

Having our own ministry became a blessing. It wasn't just the weight gain—Josie had to move around with a fifty-foot oxygen tube. It was inconvenient, but we were happy. People were maturing spiritually. We were no longer bound by religious systems controlled by jealousy and emotionalism disguised as the Holy Spirit. I was tired of being disrespected by leaders who rejected truth when it stared them in the face.

In our church, people were free to question anything they didn't understand. But inside of me, a deep yearning grew stronger. Something was missing. It felt like my soul was speaking, but I couldn't yet interpret the message. I began questioning the origins of Christianity because of the behavior of people who claimed to be "born again." The scriptures say you will know them by their fruits—their words and actions.

Josie's condition became my priority. She couldn't drive or travel easily with the oxygen tank. Her physician's office gave us a form to apply for a portable wheelchair and portable oxygen setup, but she was denied because of my income. I couldn't believe it. I called the agency myself. I asked who made these policies and what government official decided a person's health needs could be denied because of their spouse's income. They couldn't give me an answer. I felt hollow—and bitterness toward the system grew within me. A week after Josie passed she received a letter stating she was approved for the portable oxygen tank and electric chair. That notice pissed me off.

Josie felt my frustration before she passed. She reminded me to trust God.

Even with her health declining, our love never wavered. Josie and I talked about my availability, because so many things kept pulling me away from home. She came up with the idea of choosing a night just for us—Friday.

It went so well she added Saturday, Friday nights was our date night. I had to give up many outside commitments, and people became angry with me. But those nights with her were priceless. Cornelius struggled to keep the grandchildren from interrupting our date night which we did for a year before she added Saturday night.

I gave up everything for Josie because she proved her love for me by respecting me as a man.

The Moorish conference calls were every Friday for two hours. I was also driving to Charlotte, N.C., on Sundays, attending local Moorish meetings, I was the assistant coach of girls youth basketball, and training at the dojo—which was over ten miles from home. I started feeling uncomfortable being that far away in case Josie needed me.

At the time, I was a brown belt preparing for black belt training. Josie and I talked about the dedication required, and I knew I couldn't give it the focus it deserved any more. She told me that since I'd already come that far, I should finish the final year. But inside, I didn't want to, because I knew it would create a loyalty battle between my training and caring for her.

I met with Sensei Gardner and told him I couldn't commit to training for the black belt promotion—not the way I should. I told him I was putting my family first. He told me not to quit but to refocus. I said I wasn't quitting—I was choosing my wife's health and my peace of mind. I agreed to complete the training, but I couldn't train in the evenings anymore because no one would be home with Josie.

I worked full-time doing autopsies and lab work. Josie's condition worsened, and we couldn't find anyone to stay with her during the day. I was forced to retire early without reaching retirement age or completing my work years, therefore the IRS penalized my 401(k) as if they had earned the money. That's when I realized we weren't free in America. We were living under a colonial, corporate system never designed for African people—foreign to this land. My people were already here, yet that history was erased from our consciousness.

I wrote to the IRS demanding to know what my tax money was being used for, and informing them I did not consent to being taxed as a native American and not a federal employee. I wasn't waiting on a response that wasn't going to come.

I leaned on peace of mind, value, truth, and the pure love of God to carry me through what I knew was theft through an imperial system of control.

I retired because no one could stay with Josie during the day. Nyaree's schedule changed, and she could no longer visit in the mornings. I told Sensei Gardner I had to stop training during the day as well. I had to retire from karate entirely. That angered my teachers and classmates, who labeled me a quitter—after I earned the black belt I told Sensei I didn't want to train for.

Word eventually got back to me that someone in the class started a rumor saying I quit therefore I could start teaching my own class, which had to be approved by the karate organization. I didn't have any such class.

On the first day of my retirement, I was washing dishes  looking through the kitchen window admiring the back yard, realizing that for the first time in our marriage, it was just the two of us living in our home. Family and friends always stayed with us. As I enjoyed the quiet morning, I heard a faint voice calling me from Josie's room.

As I walked in, I was shocked by what I saw and smelled. Josie hadn't made it to the restroom in time. She used every bit of energy she had just to breathe, control her bowels, and get herself there. She made it—but by the time she did, her bed, nightgown, rug, restroom floor, toilet, and sink were all soiled. It was a mess.

Josie was sitting on the toilet trying to clean herself with soap and water, she was having a difficult time trying to clean herself. As soon as she saw me, she apologized for "shitting up the place." I said, "Woman, shut up. I get paid to clean shit every day—I may as well clean yours for free. You don't need to apologize. I'm glad I'm here." We laughed while I cleaned her up, removed her gown, and washed the sink and floor. I joked, "You missed the whole toilet, it's empty!" She shot back, "Aww, shut the hell up!"

We turned a terrible moment into something we were grateful for. Had I not retired that day, she wouldn't have been able to call anyone. She would've endured that alone. While she waited in the clean restroom, I pulled up the carpet and replaced her bedding. Thankfully, the mattress wasn't soiled. Once everything was clean, I helped her back into bed.

As we sat, talked, and ate breakfast, she told me one of the most profound things she ever said. Before her sickness, she couldn't get her mind to rest. She was at peace, but always had to stay busy—why she came to bed late, why she always had to find something to do, why she was constantly on the go when she could still drive. Now that she couldn't do what she used to, she had to refocus her mind according to her abilities.

She said she was thankful for the disease because it made her mind calmer and freer, even though her body felt terrible. That hit me hard. I asked her how.

She said she thanked God for me and for what we were learning from Sister Victoria's I AM teachings—along with our biblical foundation, church involvement, Tai Chi, prayer, meditation, new age teachings, smooth jazz, worship music, and the spiritual identity we've had since birth. She said she loved me deeply for being there for her, and that I was the best husband for her life because she would've had to experience that life regardless if I were there or not.

I needed income. I'd been out of work for a month, and we had to live off savings for two months. Therefore I created an exercise program called Ippon Mind and Body Training, which taught moving meditation and stretching with something I called an energy rod—designed for inner healing, not karate. Each rod came in different sizes and chakra colors representing the seven centers of spiritual power within the human body.

After going through all of that, I didn't hear from my dojo family anymore. I believed I was no longer welcome. They labeled me a quitter. I trained karate for healing—mainly for my neck and back pain. Healing was always my purpose, for myself and others. Mr. Gardner taught me karate technique, but he also taught me life.

One day, as a surprise test, Sensei Gardner told me to stand in front of the class. I thought I was going to spar, but instead he told me to get a sheet of copy paper, place it on the floor, and stand on it. Then he asked if I had advanced. I said no sir. He told me to get another sheet, put it on top of the first, and stand on both. I realized it wasn't a physical test. I looked down and said, "My feet aren't on the floor anymore."

Sensei said, "True. But you need to understand something else. Never despise small achievements. Even though the paper is thin, if you keep advancing—even a little—you're still moving forward. Everything has small beginnings. Keep adding paper, and eventually you'll be standing on a stack. That progress is obvious, but the first sheet doesn't look like anything to the eye."

I told him I could still feel the floor. He said, "You are judged by your feelings. Your emotions can stop your progress if you despise your smallest accomplishments. One sheet makes a whole pack. Strive to be whole, Mr. Bey. Never think you are less than what you can become—even if it takes time."

Sensei Gardner was a blessing. He helped me understand that even a thin sheet meant I was no longer standing on the floor. He taught me not to fear stepping beyond tradition and to use courage when I didn't understand something. He saw the character of all his students, even when I struggled to relax with everything going on that no one at the dojo knew about.

Josie was my priority, but I was also driving to Charlotte for Moorish and law classes on Sundays, attending ministry and meditation sessions, selling life insurance, learning Tai Chi, and joining Moorish conference calls every Friday while coaching girls youth basketball. One day, Josie told me all of it was pulling too much time away from her. She said things had to change once I started back to work.

She cut the conference calls, karate classes, the ministry meetings held at our home, and the long drives to Charlotte. She didn't trust the law-class teachers; she believed they just wanted money—and she turned out to be correct.

I gave it all up. We made Friday nights our date night. After six months, she told me she wanted

Saturday nights too. I said, "What?" She said, "You heard me." We enjoyed movies, food, wine coolers, the music I recorded, massages, and yes—passionate sex, her favorite thing and whatever she wanted. We enjoyed those date nights for two years.

During that time, we talked about her passing. She joked that if I remarried, she'd leave heaven and choke me. We laughed, but we made an agreement: no hospitalization or life-saving lines if her condition worsened.

One day, an official from a reputable organization made a verbal threat on my life because of his jealousy. He moved to Columbia with his grandmother, she was in her eighties and had severe arthritis. They had no food, so I bought groceries for them. As he unpacked the bags, he cried, saying no one had ever done that for them. His grandmother came out with tears in her eyes too, saying she had never seen such kindness.

I became friends with him and his grandmother for about a year. He held a black belt in Kung Fu and he had a photographic memory. We traveled to conferences and held sessions in local African stores. I helped them move into a better rental house. Grandma was full of wisdom and treated me like a son. While the official was on a conference call, I checked on Grandma. She wanted to sit in her chair. Before I helped her, she told me she was happy to see me and loved talking to me. She told me about her life, her faith in Jesus Christ , and how strong she had to be in her younger years.

She said when I came by, it brightened her day. She said I was the only Moor she knew who had Jesus' kindness. She said she got lonely because her grandson was always busy with Government things. She whispered things she wanted off her chest. She told me her grandson wasn't an honest man then she told me not to allow anyone to change my spirit.

Grandma had good days and bad ones. One day, I stopped for a normal visit and found her having one of her worst. She was weak, barely able to speak, but she perked up when she saw me. As I spoke with her, the official suddenly interrupted us and accused me—right in front of her—of having sex with his grandmother. Her face showed pure shock and hurt.

He told me he'd kill me if he ever caught me around her again. I stood up and told him I'd defend myself against him or anybody, and not to mistake kindness for weakness. Then I remembered what Minister Davis taught me: never challenge a man in his own home. Leave, and use it as testimony if he rejects your peace. This is my testimony against that wicked spirit.

I told Grandma I didn't appreciate the accusation, and she agreed—it was evil. She defended me even in her weak state. But I walked out to avoid his trap. Her face was full of sadness as I left.

Later that day, the official called to apologize. Grandma had rebuked him hard and told her family what he'd done. I knew because his son visited the next week and asked if I had been having sex with Grandma. I asked him how anyone could believe something so absurd—an eighty-year-old woman with arthritis and failing health? He knew it was a lie and said his father lived a questionable life. He spread that lie to his family that lived out of state to justify his evil practices.

A few months later, a woman considering a move to Columbia visited the official. She wanted a job in health care, so he called me to help. I gave her the contact information she needed. She was intelligent and seemed to know what she wanted as an occupation.

The next day, the official told me she liked me enough to be my "side chick." I told him I wasn't that kind of man, especially with a sick wife at home. He asked, "How's your wife gonna find out?" That told me everything I needed to know. I told him that would destroy the trust and harmony Josie and I built over thirty years. I left his home and never looked back.

A few months later, he called to tell me Grandma had passed and the coroner ordered an autopsy. I told him it was an honor to care for her body. We performed her autopsy that morning.

In March, it snowed. Josie sat in her wheelchair wrapped in a blanket, watching our grandchildren play on the deck. She asked me to push her outside. I told her the chair might get stuck, so we watched from the open back door instead. The snow was beautiful. Josie knew she wouldn't see another snowy day—I could see it in her eyes. Her skin was pale, and something in her spirit felt different.

A few weeks later, I came home from work and knew immediately something was wrong. Josie wasn't herself. She was quiet, inactive, and cold under her blanket. Later that evening, all the grandchildren were home waiting for their dad. Josie called me to help her sit up. Her heart rate was so high I could see the artery in her neck pounding like it would burst through her neck.

She told me to call an ambulance. I asked if she was sure, then she snapped, "Don't ask questions—call the ambulance now." I told the grandchildren to stay in the den and watch TV while I got ready to take her to the ER. Deep down, I knew she wasn't coming home. Every step I took felt like the last we'd ever take together.

The EMS and Columbia Fire Department arrived within fifteen minutes. They took one look at her and knew she was in trouble. She answered their questions calmly. When they asked how she felt, she said cold and weak. They saw the artery in her neck pulsing and exchanged looks—they had to move quickly. They asked which hospital to take her to, and I said Providence downtown. The firemen lifted her onto the stretcher.

As they rolled her out, I grabbed her belongings and followed them. When they loaded her into the ambulance, I had the bright idea to drive ahead of them. I figured they'd pass me before I reached the stop sign two blocks away. But when I stopped and checked my mirror, there were no emergency lights behind me. Where are they? Something felt wrong.

I turned around. On my way back, I saw the ambulance just leaving our street. Their delay made no sense. Then they turned right—heading toward Fort Jackson, where there was no ER for civilians. I followed half a block behind, yelling in my car, where the hell are y'all taking my wife? If they'd turned left, they would've been in front of the VA Hospital in five minutes. Instead, they took a long, pointless route that added seven minutes to the trip.

I watched their lights flash as they sped ahead. But when I passed the VA Hospital, their lights were gone. I assumed they had driven so fast they left me behind. I kept going to Providence Hospital's ER—about ten miles from the VA. It was around 3:00 AM. As I approached, I noticed there were no ambulances outside. A heavy feeling hit me.

Inside, I asked the receptionist where they had taken Mrs. Pittman. She said they hadn't received an ambulance in the last fifteen minutes and asked if I was sure she'd been brought there. I said yes, but I'd lost them on the way. She said, "Wait here—I'll call dispatch." A few minutes later, she told me dispatch needed to speak with me. I developed a sinking feeling in my stomach .

The dispatcher asked who he was speaking with. I said I'm Mrs. Pittman's husband.

She said Josie had an episode before they could get her into the ambulance, so the crew took her to the closest emergency room—the VA Hospital on Garners Ferry Road.

I asked, "Are you telling me she passed away?"

She said, "I'm sorry to inform you, but she was dead on arrival."

My mind fell into a state of confusion. For the first time in our marriage, I was too far away from her when she needed me most. We didn't want the staff trying to revive her. She wanted to go in peace. She didn't want to pass away at home with the grandchildren there. She held on until she got outside. She controlled her passing, just like she controlled everything she could.

I parked at the VA Hospital around 3 AM. The entrance was closed and silent. I had no idea how to get in. I walked from the front to the back, trying to find my way to her. I felt lonely and lost. I called Cornelius and Philnesha to tell them their mother had passed. They cried as I told them I still couldn't find the emergency room. I asked them to call Lisa.

The morning was still and quiet. No cars. No people. The sky was covered with stars, and the moon was bright, the early morning was warm and calm. Josie would've loved it—she always loved the heavens. As I headed toward the emergency area, a police car approached. I waved it down and told the officer, "My wife passed away, I need to get inside." He showed me the way.

I had been locked outside for twenty minutes before I finally reached her. When I saw her lying still and peaceful, I knew her suffering was over—no more struggling to breathe, no more pain that kept her from driving for two years.

The Deputy Coroner already arrived and was writing her report when the nurse brought me in. We knew each other from doing autopsies. She looked up, shocked.

"Osaze! What are you doing here? Do you know Mrs. Pittman?"

I said, "Yes. She's my wife."

She began crying and hugged me, saying she hadn't known because our last names were different. After a few minutes, she asked if I wanted time alone with Josie. I said yes.

Looking at her body, I saw the struggle was gone. She was finally at rest. Even though she was gone, her love for me was still in the room. I remembered how we grew together as a family should—how she helped me grow into a righteous man, husband, and father. I had no father figure, and she walked with me through every step of learning. She was a virtuous woman.

She chose me as I was and taught me how to love myself when I had no identity. I always felt goodness and peace inside me, but I didn't know how to accept it. My whole life, I'd had to fight for my peace of mind. Josie loved that peace. She protected it. She respected me—not just as a man, but as a spiritual man loved by Yeshua.

If we ever disagreed, she made sure we never went to sleep angry. "Sleep won't be peaceful," she'd say, "and it will show the next morning if you care for one another. Never lay your head on your pillow with anger on your tongue. The tongue is an unruly thing—who can tame it?"

Josie lived those values, even during her illness. Her children rose early to embrace her, not run from her. She made clothes with her hands, fed the hungry, supported her friends, and lived with unwavering love for Yeshua and her husband. Her husband was known throughout the city as a righteous man, a warrior for truth, a man who sought to bring well-being to those who deserved it. Josie took care of her home. She was a wonderful mother and a wonderful person.

Her favorite scriptures were Psalm 119 and Proverbs 31:10–31, and anyone who knew her would agree her life reflected those verses.

These thoughts ran through my mind as I spent my final moments with her. What a woman. I'm grateful to have known her, and grateful for the life we shared—helping others heal.

# Chapter 17 – My Reward

This chapter is my reward for the suffering I've endured—suffering this book can't fully contain. It wasn't physical suffering; it was spiritual warfare. It was the weight of godly principles planted in me from birth, and my lifelong fight to surrender my will to them—to act in harmony with what I knew was right. I endured for the Kingdom of God within me. It's written, "And from the days of John the Baptist until now the kingdom of God suffers violence, and the violent take it by force." (Matthew 11:12).

I didn't understand why my whole being leaned so strongly toward Biblical truth—why I craved understanding over empty knowledge. That desire pushed me to mature as a living soul, not a slave to religious or political systems. I had to adapt and grow from within. And I put more suffering on myself than any person ever could.

That's why I thank Yeshua for Brennan Guy—a godly man whose unconditional love for people helped shape me to value people without condition. He kept me humble by teaching me—sometimes without saying a word—what I needed to understand about myself and others. His wife, Linda, was just as diligent in righteousness. Brennan was the smartest X-ray mechanic I ever knew and a retired U.S. Air Force man. I haven't seen him in fifteen years; a coworker told me he moved to Hilton Head, S.C. But his light still shines in my mind. Be mindful of what you do to souls—nurture or injure. Brennan nurtured mine and blessed my entire family.

The stories in this chapter are for the glory of God—not to expose anyone but myself, for the sake of healing. As I grew into my purpose, I revisited the nightmares of my childhood in my thoughts. I remembered the faces in those dreams—faces I once thought were demons.

The Holy Spirit revealed they weren't demons at all; they were people I would meet later in life. The dream about the snakes represented the spirit of the people I was going to have to work with and be in church with, however their bites (state of mind) couldn't poison me but I could feel their sting which was the stress they placed upon me.

People make choices. Their choices create the fear or peace they carry. Evil doesn't choose people, people choose its energy. Evil can't lord over people unless they surrender to it.

To be effective spiritually, you must understand simplicity and timing. While I made mistakes throughout my life, something in me stayed pure—not perfect, but pure. I did things teenagers do, but I never wanted to manipulate, deceive, injure, or lie on anyone for my gain. If I ever crossed that line, I felt a deep sorrow inside, and I hated that feeling. That sorrow proved I still cared. People who choose the opposite get emotional reactions too—but they enjoy them because of the physical rewards they bring which they want last.

My reward came during a weeklong revival at Forest Drive Baptist Church, where we were members at the time. Forest Drive wasn't a traditional Baptist church; it leaned Pentecostal or Charismatic—seeking the direction of the Holy Spirit and longing for something like the Azusa Street Revival of 1906 led by William J. Seymour. Seymour prayed for hours daily and sought a Pentecostal movement filled with spontaneous worship, tongues, sanctification, healing, and unity between black and white believers. But that revival ended the way many moves of God end—racial division and internal conflict.

Forest Drive had similar diversity, and its leaders hoped to unite white and black churches to break division. They organized a large tent revival with many congregations. But like Azusa, it collapsed under confusion—arguments over tongues, internal struggles, and division. At the time, I was a Deacon, musician, and member of the worship dance team.

I spoke up when things didn't line up with God's word. I spoke privately with a few Elders and the Pastor. One Caucasian Elder received my words with humility and rejoiced, knowing they came from above. He prayed for me. The African Elder rejected them and accused me of wanting attention. I reminded him Scripture commands us to go to our leaders when confusion enters the house of God.

The main issue was speaking in tongues. I told them many were moving in a false spirit. The African American leader I knew personally rejected my words out of jealousy. Jealousy isn't racial—it's universal. It's not born to destroy; it's an energy that can make us whole if we choose correctly.

I explained that at Pentecost, people heard their own native languages spoken by foreigners—meaning it was understood. When tongues are given, there must be an interpreter, and the interpreter must be examined. Without those conditions, the gift should stop. Most churches were ignoring Scripture. I told them their desire for spiritual growth would be blocked because the Spirit of Yeshua is the Spirit of Truth. I didn't go to them to obtain recognition because I went alone without telling anyone. I went because I cared for God's people and he equipped me to speak to them. My words were rejected by all of them except for Elder Buddy Welch.

I was rejected because I wasn't part of their program—just a "nobody" to them. Some wanted to silence me simply because the message didn't come through them. I told them if the word had come to them, there would've been no problem proclaiming it. Then I left. See Acts 2:1–21, 1 Corinthians 14:27–28, and Isaiah 28:10–13 (KJV).

My reward came sometime between 1996 and 2000 during that tent revival. I don't recall the exact year. I was learning to meditate, to seek heaven from within, and to love myself despite a lifetime blueprint of rejection. I wondered how Yeshua (Christ) could use me with my memory issues. The principles of Love, Truth, Peace, Freedom, and Justice were already part of my nature—but I had to accept them. That acceptance became the true revival within me.

"Blessed are the pure in heart, for they shall see God." "The kingdom of God is within you." (Matthew 5:8; Luke 17:21).

My first spiritual vision happened in the chapel of a local medical organization while my friend

Mike Belz was praying across the room. I loved the Spirit's presence during worship. I began singing about the power, beauty, and splendor of the Creator—the One whose voice makes angels tremble. I worshiped uninterrupted for about ten minutes.

With my eyes closed, the entire room suddenly filled with brightness which was glorious. I fell to my knees, face to the floor. The brightness consumed everything. The floor felt like it vanished beneath me. Then I saw a throne—and the One sitting on it—though my eyes were still closed tight. The body on the throne was brighter than the sun. I knew immediately who He was. I cried out, "I see Jesus! I see Jesus!" It felt like an hour in His presence, though it was only minutes. I heard nothing—just saw glory.

Once I stood, I told Mike what happened and asked if he saw anything. He said no—only heard my voice and feared for me because I was trembling. I told only Josie and Pastor Glen Anderson about the vision. I was confused why I was chosen to see that and prayed daily for answers. Every time I closed my eyes, I saw the brightness until it slowly faded.

The second vision happened after a tent revival service. The speaker taught about prayer and meditation—going within for answers, focusing on the desires of your heart, having faith, and maintaining a pure heart. I was excited because I was already experiencing what he described.

When I closed my eyes, I began worshiping within my thoughts, focusing on God's beauty and power. Suddenly, I was on a high mountain unlike anything on earth. The flowers and trees were breathtaking, it was like being in an animated movie, it was beauty beyond my imagination. Then I heard a voice call my name: "Phillip, come to the edge."

The voice was like thunder. The man stood over seven feet tall, bronze, radiant, with thick dark hair and a garment the color of deep violet. He motioned to me again: "Phillip, don't be afraid. Come to the edge." I told him I was afraid, yet something within me compelled me forward. With each step, my fear faded.

When I reached the edge, he disappeared. I looked down and saw a great valley with a glorious city rising upward, filled with power I could feel through my body—crystals and gold shimmering on every rooftop. Then the speaker ended the meditation session. I stayed in my seat and told no one except Josie afterward. She was disappointed because she believed sharing it would bless others.

She encouraged me to meet with Pastor Anderson, so we did. When I told him, he looked astonished and said, "Brother, we all know you're an unusual person who loves the Lord. Your vision is fascinating—I'm jealous." I asked what it meant. He admitted he didn't know, only that it was for me alone and I shouldn't tell anyone else. He was right—they couldn't give me answers.

Josie urged me to stop seeking validation from men and trust God. I did. One evening during prayer, the mountain vision returned, and I understood its meaning: I was being shown how to overcome fear. The angel knew I feared heights. He taught me that fear must be faced while it's still present. Courage is taking steps while trembling. That's how you walk through the fire and allow hope and truth to be your guide.

The chapel vision revealed His glory—the fullness of His coming, his power and might. Only the pure in heart can see God. I didn't need to be perfect, but I had to love others unconditionally, which requires courage and wisdom. That love is for people, not the negative choices they make.

My reward wasn't material. It was spiritual. These visions were given so I could tell this generation that heaven is real—its beginnings are within us. I can't tell you about the fear of hell, but I can tell you about the existence of heaven because I revere the most high God. Other worlds and beings exist beyond what this world is allowed to understand because nations—made up of individual hearts—choose their own moral path that can't line up with the universe.

Those visions were for me because I would value them as my ancestors valued theirs by choosing to live a life of righteousness and developing a love for the most high. I learned to seek and apply wisdom. It's like pouring warm oil into the mind keeping it lubricated enough to avoid the frictions life brings.

This book is in honor of my family members that suffered daily knowing the disease was thriving through their brain and body, they experienced what I thought I had which inflicted fear within me. I can't imagine what the fear would be like to actually have it. Their suffering was not for the kingdom of heaven, however their brave acceptance of it was through their positive thoughts and actions which was blessed by the Creator. Their reward will be mighty because of how they lived without blaming God or people as they were drawn to him with love. Thanks to Reatha Pittman, Billy Pittman, Joseph Pittman and John Pittman. They fought the good fight of faith and wisdom. I learned to seek and apply wisdom. Like pouring warm oil into the mind, I keep it lubricated enough to avoid the frictions life brings. They treasured the wisdom of life within them, living with that disease was better than not experiencing life at all.

The following page is a photo honoring my late siblings who lived a life we can't imagine as they carried a hidden disease. I wanted to be them but instead I was chosen to serve them. They were all powerful men. Seated bottom row from left to right: Joseph Pittman and Billy Pittman. Back row from left to right: John Pittman, Floyd Mitchell Pittman and Osaze Bey (Phillip Pittman-age 16).

**Breaking The Chains of Fear for Self-Healing**


Library of Congress Control Number: 2026906710



This book is published by:
**Da Wolf's Pray Lo Radio**
**803-414-4440**
dainnerhealinggym@gmai.com

In association with
**Professional Printers, Inc.**
301-B Greystone Boulevard
Columbia, SC 29210
803-796-4000, Ext. 312 (Office)
803-331-5534 (Cell)
hmurphy@proprinters.com

**ISBN:** 979-8-234-10742-0

Cover design by: Osaze Bey and Princellia Conna Hampton
Interior layout by: Diamond Johnson

Printed in the United States of America.

This publication is distributed by (Professional Printers, Inc.).

The information contained in this book is provided for educational and informational purposes only and is not intended as medical, psychological, or therapeutic advice. The author and publisher disclaim any liability arising directly or indirectly from the use or application of the contents of this book.

## Breaking The Chains of Fear for Self-Healing

### By Osaze Bey (Phillip Pittman)

This book consists of 17 chapters, stories of my life revealing the origin of my fear through my environments as a child. Fear gained control by the negative blueprint which was the mindset of other people developed within their own environment by negative dominance. I suffered mentally as a child because I was born with a short memory. I hated myself. I was forgetful when it came to numbers and reading. I believed I was going to die before I became a teenager because of a hereditary disease. Self-healing began once I became conscious of loving myself. Pure love will provide endurance. Truth will provide you the power to stand with courage. The value of self will create harmony for positive consequences. This book will activate every emotion, you will smile, laugh, cry, love, experience jealousy, envy, hate, sadness, and feel happiness.

www.ingramcontent.com/pod-product-compliance
Lightning Source LLC
LaVergne TN
LVHW050633100826
845148LV00011B/1851

* 9 7 9 8 2 3 4 0 1 7 4 2 0 *